THE DEFINITION OF PSYCHOLOGY

SECOND EDITION

THE DEFINITION
OF PSYCHOLOGY

FRED S. KELLER
Western Michigan University

NEW YORK
APPLETON–CENTURY–CROFTS
EDUCATIONAL DIVISION
MEREDITH CORPORATION

PREFACE TO THE SECOND EDITION

This book was first written as a brief introduction to the history of systematic psychology as we knew it in the middle '30s of this century. The present revision reflects, directly and indirectly, some of the important happenings since then. A chapter has been added, for example, on learning theories and radical behaviorism, and, as a backdrop for this development, material has been included on the history of the conditioned reflex, the law of effect, and the criteria of mind.

In addition, I have included, as a kind of penance, a chapter on Freud and McDougall; and I have repaired the earlier omission of Thomas Hobbes and H. L. F. von Helmholtz in my story.

In the 36-year gap between 1937 and 1973, changes in a person's writing style can be expected. I have attempted to avoid the appearance of a contrast in my own, but I haven't entirely succeeded. I ask the reader to be gentle.

Little books need indices, like big ones. I am very grateful to my son, John V. Keller, for preparing the index to this.

F.S.K.

PREFACE TO THE FIRST EDITION

This book is the partial result of my attempt, during the past six years, to provide college students with an introductory course of instruction in psychology that will serve at once as an orientation for those who expect to go no further into the field and as a pre-view for those who plan to concentrate therein. The material here presented has been selected with the aim of leading the beginner along a portion of the route that psychology's fathers and founders traveled on the way to the modern problem of defining and systematizing the science. In my own teaching practice this material constitutes the first part of the course-work and is followed regularly by an outline treatment of four major fields—animal, child, differential, and abnormal psychology—a text on which is now in preparation. Such a mode of approach is related to my conviction that the usual beginner's text or lecture-course in psychology fails to supply an adequate conception of the developmental aspect of the province or of the breadth and variety of interest and research within it.

It will be difficult for me to repay Dr. B. F. Skinner of the University of Minnesota, Professor Clarence W. Young of Colgate, and my wife, Frances, for their encouragement and aid during the actual composition of these chapters. Without their criticism and the helpful editorial comment of Professor Elliott, many more faults might be found with the present portrayal than are now exposed.

I am grateful to Harcourt, Brace and Company, Henry Holt and Company, J. B. Lippincott Company, Liveright Publishing Corporation, Longmans, Green and Company, The Macmillan Company, W. W. Norton and Company, and Charles Scribner's Sons for permission to quote passages from their books.

Fred S. Keller

Hamilton, New York

CONTENTS

1
PHILOSOPHICAL BEGINNINGS

Long before psychology came to be treated as an experimental science there were men who interested themselves in matters that would now be called psychological. The influence of these men upon later generations has been great, and it is not strange that we should approach the problem of defining modern psychology by reference to their opinions and discoveries. In fact, it is only by so doing that we can properly appreciate the difficulty of defining psychology or evaluate the tremendous advances made in recent years.

Although our historical preparation will be limited to the mention of a mere handful of men, there were actually hundreds—perhaps thousands—whose ideas we might consider forerunners of present-day conceptions of our province. No science goes ahead by the leaps and bounds which an initial excursion into its history seems to indicate. Progress is slow, and often by tiny steps, which should be encouraging to the student who aspires to add his item to the achievements of the past.

In dealing here with the beliefs of early representative figures, the author does not mean to imply that one should subscribe to them or treat them as authoritative. Some would nowadays be called fantastic or bizarre. Their existence may have brought some problem to the focus of attention without solving it to anyone's satisfaction.

How far into the past shall we reach to pick up our historical threads? This is not an easy question to answer. We might begin with the "psychological" views of primitive man, especially with his beliefs concerning the "ghost-soul," but our factual footing would be none too secure at such a distance. Or we might start with a more articulate age—with Aristotle (384–322 B.C.) of ancient Greece, the true father of all psychology; with Claudius Galen (c. 130–199 A.D.), the Roman physician whose classification of temperaments and localization of reason in the brain foreshadowed much of modern doctrine and research; with Thomas Aquinas (1224–1275), the voice of the medieval church in many psychological matters. None of these, however, is as directly and immediately in line with our present concern as the French philosopher and mathematician, René Descartes (1596–1650)—as exciting a figure, personally and intellectually, as one may hope to uncover in turning the pages of a history book.

Born of the lesser nobility, trained in a Jesuit school, a soldier for a time (by some accounts not above the "excesses of youth"), and, finally, a scholar of high rank and radical opinions—the story of this man's life might easily divert us from the main track of our interest. We must, therefore, content ourselves here with a brief treatment of the reasons which rightfully entitle him to be called the Father of Modern Psychology.

René Descartes was the first great *dualist* among the world's philosophers. He was the first to make a sharp distinction between *mind* and *body*—a distinction which has made no little trouble for psychologists down to the present day. Furthermore, he was that kind of a dualist which we call an *interactionist*—that is, he believed that the mind may affect the body and the body the mind.

Descartes' views were nearly identical with the "commonsense" opinion of most of the persons who will read this account—proof convincing enough of his influence upon the thought of later generations. The mind, to Descartes, was that which "thinks"; the principal site of its activity was in the head; and it could take up no physical space. The body, on the other hand, was a clearly objective "extended substance," mechanical in its action and obeying all the known laws of the inanimate. Animals, indeed, having no minds or souls (the two terms were synonymous to Descartes), were considered to be nothing more than machines.

The hypothesis advanced by Descartes to explain the interaction of mind and body was, if inaccurate, at least ingenious and in some accord with the existing views of the functions of the human nervous system. As an illustration we may consider one phase of this speculation—that which concerns the manner of the mind's influence upon the body.

The sensory nerves of the body, for Descartes, were tubes containing filaments (likened by him to bell-ropes) which conveyed the influence of the external world to the central "cavern" or ventricle of the brain; the motor nerves were also treated as tubes, but ones in which the "animal spirits" (blood vapors), arising from the heart, passed from the central cavern out to the muscles, producing bodily movement.[1] Thus, an excitation of a sense organ would cause a tugging on the bell-rope which, at its central termination, would open tiny valves in the ends of nearby motor nerves, permitting the spirits to flow into the appropriate muscles, causing the latter to swell and shorten, thereby moving the bones.

But what of the influence of the mind? Descartes' answer was direct, if not plausible. His argument was that the soul or mind, being unitary, must influence the body, which has two symmetrical halves, through the agency of some single structure shared by both body halves. The structure that he chose was the pineal body, a small gland of the brain that, for him, projected into the turbulent vapors of the central cavern. The movement of this structure, at the mind's command, was supposed to be capable of changing the spirit flow and interrupting the usual sequence of activity; the soul's desire was thus translated into bodily motion and interaction was achieved.

Descartes made other contributions, some of which will be mentioned in connection with other problems and the thoughts of other men, but none have proved quite so exasperating theoretically as these general conceptions of dualism and interactionism. We shall

[1] "Sensory" and "motor," as the reader may know, are the terms applied respectively to those nerves which carry impulses from the sense-organs to the brain or spinal cord and from the brain or cord to the motor organs, e.g., the muscles.

see this clearly further along when we consider the views of later "systematists" in psychology.

John Locke (1632–1704), the British philosopher, became interested in psychological matters through a friendly discussion of the nature and acquisition of knowledge. At that time he undertook to write a very brief statement of his views with respect to this problem. Twenty years later he published the book that resulted from his attempt, *An Essay Concerning Human Understanding*—a book that can still be a source of quiet delight for the unhurried reader.

It is in this book that we find a development of the theme, at that time rather radical, that "all ideas come from experience." Locke compared the mind in its virginal state to a sheet of white paper upon which experience writes. He said: "Let us suppose the mind to be, as we say, white paper, void of all characters, without any ideas; how comes it to be furnished . . . ? To this I answer, in one word, from experience."

This view is not really a new one historically. Even Aristotle had spoken of the mind as initially a blank tablet (*tabula rasa*). But the development of the view is Locke's own; and it came at a very appropriate time. Descartes, and others, had argued for "innate" ideas—ideas especially clear and belonging to the mind by virtue of no influence of the outside world.

In taking his position, elaborating it, and defending it with page on page of careful analysis and direct appeal to his own experience, John Locke inaugurated a movement in philosophy now known as "English empiricism," which has had such widespread effect that we hardly recognize its presence in our thinking nowadays. Without it, however, the rise of modern observational and experimental psychology, of which we are so proud, might well have been delayed for many years.

An *idea*, to Locke, was "whatever it is which the mind can be employed about in thinking." Whiteness, hardness sweetness, man, motion, drunkenness, elephant, army, and thinking—all these were mentioned by him as typical ideas, and all might be considered to come from one of two sources: directly, from the senses, or indirectly, from the mind's reflection upon the sense-knowledge—ideas, and ideas about ideas!

Furthermore, Locke considered that ideas might be simple or complex, the latter being really compounds of the former and reducible to them, upon careful analysis. Thus, if to the idea of substance "be joined the simple idea of a certain dull whitish colour, with certain degrees of weight, hardness ductility, and fusibility, we have the idea of lead," a complex idea. In this way Locke threw a bone of contention far into the future, for, as we shall see, the possibility of analyzing the human mind into elements, as well as the probable nature of these elements, has been a hotly debated issue in more recent years. Locke's immediate successors carried these notions of analysis and compounding to regrettable extremes, and the reaction has been vigorous.

Since Locke has often been labeled "the first associationist" it may be well to include here a mention of the fact that the most generally used term to describe the combination and compounding of ideas is "association." Locke himself used the phrase "association of ideas" as a chapter heading in the *Essay,* but it was left to his followers to give it the stress that has embedded it so firmly in our own everyday vocabularies.

One more distinction made by Locke may serve as a good introduction to the teachings of the next philosopher on our list: the distinction made between what he called the "primary" and "secondary" qualities of objects, which we may treat as a difference between ideas. Briefly stated, it is this: some simple ideas of sense resemble the objects of the external world which cause them; other simple ideas of sense, although caused by such objects, do not resemble them. For example, ideas of solidity, figure, and motion are like the external objects; but ideas of colors, sounds, or tastes are *un*like anything in the objects which arouse them.

We need not bother ourselves with his reasons for dividing simple ideas of sense into these two groups, but it may be pointed out that here was a recognition by Locke that our perceptions of the world, at least in some cases, may not be mirror-pictures of the world itself—a view similar to that of a famous physiologist in later times, who argued that we are not directly aware of the objects of sense but of the nerves that lie between the objects and our minds!

Thomas Hobbes (1588–1679), another Briton, who lived in the days of Descartes and Locke, is said to have been disliked by both, for his views on philosophy and government respectively. Interested mainly in political theory, he was also steeped in classical studies and well acquainted with the science of his time. Under the influence of Galileo Galilei, to whom he paid a visit in 1636, he came to the conclusion that human "sense," human thought, and human motives could be reduced to a physical common denominator—*motion*. "All that exists" said he, "is matter; all that occurs is motion."

In *sensing*, for example, an external object "presseth the organ proper to each sense"; this "pressure" is transmitted by the nerves to the brain and to the heart. (From the latter organ comes a "counter pressure," which leads a person to localize the object as "outside.") *Imagination*, he argues, is simply "decaying sense"—motion, strong or weak, that continues in the brain when the stimulus-object is no longer present to excite. This distinction between the sensed and the imaginal, which we saw in Locke's "ideas of sensation" and "ideas of reflection," has plagued students of psychology down to the present day.

Hobbes, like Locke, was an *empiricist*; there are those who have even called him the father of the doctrine. In the *Leviathan* (1651), his best-known work, he says that "there is no conception in man's mind, which hath not at first, totally or by parts, been begotten upon the organs of sense. The rest are derived from that original." He was also an *associationist*, and talks about "Traynes of Thought" in which one "Imagination" follows another in the same order as that of the sense objects from which they were derived: "those motions that immediately succeeded one another in the sense, continue also together after sense."

In treating such associations, Hobbes brings in a new idea. Some trains of thought are *guided* by desire or purpose; others are *"Unguided, without Designe* . . . and seem impertinent to one another, as in a Dream." Here is recognition, at an early date, of motivating factors that govern human action; but Hobbes is even clearer when he talks of *appetites* and *aversions*.

He begins with the assertion that there are two kinds of motion—*vital*, as in the case of breathing, and *voluntary*, as in speaking, moving, and "going." (Here is a distinction of which we'll hear more.) Voluntary motion, the more important of the two, appears in small beginnings of movement which may be called "endeavour"—before the "going," says Hobbes, there is the thought, "which way?" and endeavour when directed *towards* an object, is what we mean by *appetite* or *desire*; when directed "fromwards" something, it is what we call *aversion*.

This classification of motives is followed by another, with an equally modern ring. "Of appetites and aversions, some are born with men; as appetite of food, appetite of excretion . . . (which may also and more properly be called aversions, from somewhat they feel in their bodies). . . . The rest, which are appetites of particular things, proceed from experience, the triall of their effects, upon themselves, or other men."

Psychologists have honored these distinctions, even in the present century, and, like Hobbes, they have sometimes been uncertain as to the class in which a motive, either inborn or acquired, should properly be listed. It is often hard to say whether an organism, animal or human, is going *towards* something "good" or *fromwards* something "evil."

Whereas Thomas Hobbes believed that everything was matter and John Locke felt that we had a physical world and a mind that knew about it, either directly or indirectly, neither belief was shared by the equally brilliant Irishman whose views we may now consider. George Berkeley (1685–1753)—Dublin-born, a Trinity College graduate, a bishop by appointment, and a philosopher by disposition—did not believe in the existence of material substance!

Belief in mind as the only true reality, although reflected today in some philosophies and in the doctrines of special sects, is obviously not characteristic of modern common sense. The average person is more inclined to agree with Lord Byron that

> When Bishop Berkeley said "there was no matter,"
> And proved it,—'twas no matter what he said.

Nevertheless, the view, philosophically, is not at all unusual and is not as easy to disprove as its apparent absurdity would indicate. Moreover, in one form or another, it has even been taken seriously by some psychologists while searching for a definition of their science and seeking to determine its place among other sciences.

Since John Locke's secondary qualities (the colors, sounds, tastes, and so forth) showed his doubt of the existence of certain things in the outer world—at least as they were pictured in the mind—Bishop Berkeley can be said to have reached his position by going Locke one better. Berkeley denies that the mind pictures objects at all. A little thought may convince the reader of this disturbing possibility. Consider, for a moment, that the page now being read *might* not be physically "out there" at all, but only "in mind"! What is there, with absolute sureness, but so much sensation of a visual, auditory, or touch quality—certain modes of experience, so to speak—distinguished and named only through their "mental" differences?

One other, more concrete and understandable contribution of Berkeley is always mentioned by historians. It concerns the question how we know the distance from us to objects belonging to the world of sight. More specifically, how do we know the distance from us to this book, the picture on the wall, or the tree outside our window?

In spite of the fact that the reader may never have considered that there is a problem involved in his judgment of the distance or the solidity of seen objects—the so-called third-dimensional aspect of visual experience—it has long been a very annoying psychological problem. Leonardo da Vinci, the artist-scientist, recognized it, and so did Descartes; but it was Berkeley whose analysis was most complete and, for many years, conclusive.

Berkeley argued that we never sense visual depth, or the third dimension, directly, but always by means of *cues* or "criteria" whose meaning for such judgments we have learned to interpret; for how, he might have said, could an object-image, impressed upon the sensitive surface of our eye, tell us how far it has come—of the distance traveled before it reached that surface—any more than a letter that comes to us with its postmark blurred or missing?

In his *New Theory of Vision* (1709) Berkeley describes the probable nature of these important cues or "stamps." First of all there is the matter of relative size. A quarter of a mile away we see the figure of a friend. His image impressed upon our eyes is, we may agree, quite small. Do we, therefore, judge that we have a shrunken friend? Not at all. We see nothing unusual in his size; we see him merely *at a distance*. And what holds for our friend holds for other objects too—the larger the nearer, the smaller the farther away—so that we may say, with Berkeley, that the relative size of objects is a criterion of their distance.

Besides this there are other factors. For instance the object is judged nearer if it partially hides another from our view—the factor of "interposition"; while faint, unsaturated colors (e.g., the bluish haze of far-off mountains) are often associated with distance—the factor of "aerial perspective." Relative size, interposition, aerial perspective—all these cues were mentioned by Berkeley (in less modern terms) as aids to our judgment of distance, and all of them have been the technical property of every painter for ages.

The next criterion is, however, not so obvious. Berkeley called it an "appreciation of the distance between the pupils of the eyes"; we speak of it as "binocular convergence." When a nearby object is focused, or "fixated," the two eyes converge (in extreme cases appear crossed), and an appreciation of this convergence, in terms of sensation from the eye muscles, tells us of the distance of the object fixated—thus, the greater the convergence, the nearer the object, and vice versa.

The final criterion is that which we now call "accommodation" and explain by the change in the shape of the eyes' lenses in response to the contraction of tiny muscles attached to each. Objects very close to the eye require great contraction of these muscles; those that are three or four feet away require very little. Although unfamiliar with these details, Berkeley did recognize the influence and treated the sensations arising from such changes as another source of information relative to the distance of the looked-at object.

This highly specialized contribution is perhaps the closest to present-day psychological studies of any that I have cited. Had Berkeley made some attempt to verify his theory by appeal to a more objective and controlled experimental technique, by measurement of the conditions under whih his criteria were operative in a group of persons, we might today call him the father of experimental psychology. But had he done so it would have been an exception to the usual slow course of historical development, and we cannot demand too much of one man—especially one whose interests were philosophic rather than scientific. The surprising thing is that George Berkeley, a "subjective idealist" among philosophers, should have come as close as he did to the solution of a scientific problem that still challenges us.

Just as the inclusion of one guest at a party often demands the inclusion of others, so the temptation is very great to add many names to our list of the men who have been responsible in some important sense for present-day conceptions of our science. Perhaps, therefore, I'll be forgiven if I devote a sentence or two to each of a few more men, principally philosophers, who helped to set the psychological stage.

David Hume (1711–1776), a Scottish philosopher, historian, and statesman, did for Berkeley what Berkeley had done for Locke. To quote from a 20th century account of Hume's contributions to psychology:

> Locke had eliminated from experience all but the sense impressions and their combinations. He still accepted the existence of objects that were similar to our ideas. Berkeley went a step farther by his denial of the existence of objects at all. He found a justification for the ideas in the fact that God gave and guaranteed them . . . . Hume took the next obvious step by questioning the existence of God and the soul. This left nothing real except sensations and ideas.[2]

In addition to this, Hume made a clean-cut distinction, still prevalent, between these sensations (Hume said "impressions") and ideas (we say "images"); and he treated what we regard as "cause and effect" in our everyday world as a mere sequence of mental events occurring with such regularity and in such order as to give us the illusion that there is a necessary connection between two somethings in the objective world. The significance of these ideas will be apparent when we come to review some very recent opinions concerning the true business of the psychologist.

David Hartley (1705–1757), an English physician and scholar of Hume's generation, is credited with the development of two concepts, both of which he treated in a book bearing the homely title: *Observations on Man, His Frame, His Duty, and His Expecta-*

---

[2] W. B. Pillsbury. *The History of Psychology*, pp. 92-93.

tions (1749). The first was that of "association" (already considered by Hobbes, Locke, Berkeley, and Hume), which Hartley extended to include not only ideas but sensations and actions as well, and used to explain the nature of memory, imagination, emotion, and other complex mental states—even those pertaining to morals. The second concept was that which we now call "psychophysical parallelism," according to which sensations, ideas, and other mental events run alongside of, but are not affected by, events of a more bodily nature—specifically, physical changes in the nerves and the brain. (An earlier expression of this view had compared the mind and body to a pair of clocks, placed back to back, running in perfect time with each other but exercising no mutual influence.) Hartley was, like Descartes, a dualist, but a parallelist rather than an interactionist. Of the two views, contrary to common-sense expectation, Hartley's turned out to be the more acceptable to the majority of psychologists in later days.

James Mill (1773–1836), the son of a Scottish cobbler, was the intellectual descendant of Hartley. He made extreme use of the "association of ideas" in explaining mental life. Beginning in the usual fashion, with sensations and their copies, ideas, he pointed out in great detail how the latter may logically be connected and compounded. Just how far he went in this direction can be seen in the following classical statement from his *Analysis of the Phenomena of the Human Mind* (1829):

Not only do simple ideas, by strong association, run together, and form complex ideas: but a complex idea . . . is capable of entering into combinations with other ideas, both simple and complex . . . .

Brick is one complex idea, mortar is another complex idea; these ideas, with ideas of position and quantity, compose my idea of a wall. My idea of a plank is a complex idea, my idea of a rafter is a complex idea, my idea of a nail is a complex idea. These, united with the same ideas of position and quantity, compose my duplex idea of a floor. In the same manner, my complex idea of glass, and wood, and others, compose my duplex idea of a window; and these duplex ideas, united together, compose my idea of a house, which is made up of various duplex ideas. How many complex, or duplex ideas, are all united in the idea of furniture? How many more in the idea of merchandize? How many more in the idea called Every Thing?

John Stuart Mill (1806–1873) agreed with his father, James Mill, in attaching great importance to the principle of association in explaining complex ideas, but, unlike his father, appealed more to experience than to logic in his analysis. To James Mill a complex idea was actually supposed to *consist* of many simpler ideas, even though such ideas might escape the most careful scrutiny. John Stuart Mill argued that the simpler ideas *generate* more complex ones which are definitely more than the mere summation of the simple components. Because of this difference in theory between father and son, the former's view has often been called "mental mechanics" and the latter's "mental chemistry." Each supposed that the fundamental units of mind were sensations (as well as their copies, ideas) and these were united under certain prescribed laws of association; but John Stuart Mill was less interested in what *ought* to be found in a complex idea than in what *could* be found. Where he differed from his father he came closer to later teaching.

By this time, a certain trend should be apparent to the reader. We have seen how the mind came to be separated from the body; we have heard the argument that all ideas come from experience; we have made the distinction between sensations and ideas; and we have been told that associations may be guided by desire. In addition, we have had a glimpse of a psychological theory of *causality* (Hume); we have been given several answers to the mind-body question—interactionism (Descartes), materialism (Hobbes), idealism (Berkeley), and parallelism (Hartley); and we have found one or two specific anticipations of present-day research and theorizing.

Descartes and the "mental philosophers" played an early part in launching the young science with which we are here concerned. But much more had to be done before our modern discipline emerged. Sooner or later, these armchair ideas, no matter how insightful, had to leave the speculative realm for the world of observation and experiment. To see how this took place, we shall have to cross the English Channel and sample the researches that were taking place, especially on German soil, in the latter half of the 19th century.

2

SENSORY
PHYSIOLOGY

As we move into this new province, the stream of historical influence narrows and deepens as it becomes more scientific; and we always have to keep in mind that it is but one of several courses that we might have taken (and will go back to take, in later chapters). It is a physiological stream, comprising studies of all the senses—sight, hearing, taste, touch, and smell, as well as the newly-discovered muscle (kinesthetic) sense; it treats of the nerves that serve each organ, and even the corresponding functions of the brain.

This work was, of course, related to theories like those of Hartley and Descartes, but it went far beyond their crude imaginings of the structure and the function of the human body. It was analytical and objective, teasing out with delicate methods various details of physical change arising from the excitations of the eye, the ear, and other organs. It disclosed the speed of nerve reaction over "bell-ropes" that were smaller than the smallest that Descartes could have imagined; and it discovered special areas of the brain which were related to both muscle and sense-organ function. Many great scientists—English and French, as well as German—contributed to this widespread movement. If I mention only two of them here, it is because the aims of this little book forbid the discussion of many, and because the men selected represent sufficiently well the

13

combination of philosophic belief and natural-science discipline that was to generate psychology itself as a special field of study.

Hermann Ludwig Ferdinand von Helmholtz (1821–1894), physicist, physiologist, and, in some degree, psychologist, was a mediocre student throughout his early schooling, but managed to secure his higher education under military sponsorship, serving for seven years thereafter as a Prussian Army surgeon. From the age of 17, his interest was in physics and, even while in the Army, he managed to make important contributions to this field, becoming one of the shining lights of 19th-century science.

Among the things he did of psychological value, may be listed his monumental work on human vision, which treats the physics, the physiology, and the psychology of that sense in such detail and such extent that it remains of value today for researchers everywhere. (It was he who invented the ophthalmoscope, which makes it possible to inspect the retina of the eye, and the ophthalmometer, a very useful instrument for measuring ocular changes.) His work on hearing was equally influential and of use to students of music as well as science. It was he who clarified the function of the auditory ossicles—the "hammer," 'anvil," and "stirrup" bones within the middle ear; and it was he who developed a "resonance" theory of inner-ear function to account for several thousand different pitches that human beings can distinguish—a theory that has commanded respect for the past 100 years.

Helmholtz took account of many sensory problems which had bothered thinkers of the past, including one that the reader has already met in Hobbes, Locke, Descartes, and others. This is the question of how much of our mental life is derived from contact with the outside world and how much we bring with us. Descartes had said that certain very clear ideas were innate, known by intuition—the axioms of geometry, for example. Locke had denied this and so had the other empiricists. Helmholtz knew about the problem and sided with the British, taking an *empiristic* (often called *genetic*) point of view and arguing that geometrical axioms are simply learned relationships.

Related to such problems, Helmholtz had a theory of perception which bears resemblance to some of the older teachings (e.g., Bishop

Berkeley's) as well as some that were to come. Our experience of objects or events in the outside world, he said, includes not only simple patterns of sensation due to current stimulation but also images (ideas) derived from earlier impressions. What we perceive at any moment would therefore usually be a blend of past and present and sometimes would be more of the latter than the former. As twilight and darkness come on within a familiar room, the contribution of sensation elements decreases, while that of past experience plays an ever greater role. When total darkness comes, we find our way about in the room with the aid of memory-images alone.

Gustav Theodor Fechner (1801–1887) is best known today as "the father of quantitative psychology," yet he never intended to be a psychologist. Born in a little village of southeastern Germany, the son of a German Lutheran preacher; reared in studious surroundings and trained in medicine; subsequently a mathematician and physicist of distinction (with a flair for writing satirical poetry)–this is the story of the first half of Fechner's life. It was not, indeed, until 1850, after a serious and prolonged "nervous breakdown," that he became actively interested in the philosophical question of the mind's relation to the body–a question which led him, by virtue of his natural-science training, to experimental psychology.

We have already seen a recognition of this mind-body problem in the work of Descartes, Locke, Hobbes, Berkeley, Hume, and Hartley, but it was Fechner who saw the possibility of attacking it with the experimental method. Whether he solved it thereby is very doubtful, but in ten years of patient investigation he founded the science of *psychophysics*–the quantitative study of the relation between the mental life (Fechner dealt with sensations) and certain aspects of the physical world (stimuli).

It is not essential that we consider Fechner's psychophysics in any detail here. He made it clear once and for all that experimental techniques and mathematical procedures could be applied to psychological problems. The methods of measurement that he developed are brought into use today, in slightly modified form, whenever we try to find out anything really definite concerning the sensitivity of the human, or even animal, organism to the countless and disturbing changes of the outside world. How bright the star in order to be seen; how loud the sound to be heard; how heavy the touch to be felt? To answer these and a thousand other questions we turn to Fechner's psychophysical methods.

What has this to do with the problem of defining psychology? The answer is plain. The work of Fechner (and others) showed quite irrefutably that no matter what one's philosophical opinions might be with respect to the mind-body problem there was still the possibility of constructing an experimental psychology. Something specific about human activity (Fechner called it something *mental*) could be measured and related in an exact manner to something else (he called it *physical*). The enormous bulk of meaningful material gathered together was the result of no mere accident, nor was it the fruit of philosophical speculation. Few psychologists today are aware of Fechner's mind-body views but none can ignore his experimental findings.

And this has been the story ever since. Whatever the conclusions reached as to psychology's true subject matter, there is always that formidable and ever-growing body of scientific fact to justify the attempt at a systematic treatment. The boundaries of the sciences are never really very sharply defined, and a new field of research is not to be scorned on the basis of its temporary lack of a universally satisfying definition. Should this statement seem obscure to the reader, let him be patient; the fog will raise shortly, when we deal directly with the business of "system-making."

3

THE FOUNDING
OF OUR SCIENCE

Between "fathers" and "founders" of sciences a distinction may be made. Compare, for a moment, a science to a garden. The "fathers" plow the ground and sow the seed; the "founders" do the weeding, the watering, the transplanting, and the fencing—they care for the garden in its early growth. The seed may be dropped by countless hands, by many of them carelessly; hence there may be many fathers, each unknowing of the part he plays. But the founders must be aware that a garden is in the making, and theirs is the arduous task of nursing and tending until helpers arrive. Founders are few.

I have called Aristotle the father of psychology; Descartes the father of modern psychology; and Fechner the father of quantitative (or experimental) psychology. Other candidates for such distinctions might have been proposed. Moreover, as specialization appears in the psychological garden, ancestry is easier to identify, and more and more fathers may be named, with more justification.

Fechner may, with good reason, be called the founder of psychophysics and the father of experimental psychology; he developed the former and he showed the way to the latter. It remained, however, for another distinguished German to become the true founder of modern experimental psychology; and in the treatment of this man's achievement we approach more closely to the solution of our problem of definiton.

Wilhelm Wundt (1832–1920) was, like Fechner, the son of a German Lutheran pastor of a village parish, and also like Fechner and Helmholtz, he was trained (at the University of Heidelberg) to be a physician. Like both men too, his interests turned from the practical to the academic during his study years. Physiology, philosophy, logic, and ethics—all these fields claimed his attention at one time or another, but he was fundamentally a psychologist and, unlike Fechner, he knew it.

The time was ripe for the founding of modern psychology. Besides the intellectual legacy already mentioned, there were many contributions from other fields. Physiology donated most. Early experimental psychology was based upon physiological techniques and findings. But in addition to this and the philosophical tradition there were problems bequeathed by astronomy, anthropology, and the study of hypnotism. It remained only for a man of Wundt's caliber to weave them all into the pattern of a new psychology.

In 1873–1874, after at least fifteen years of preparation, Wundt published his *Outlines of Physiological Psychology*, called by one historian "the most important book in the history of modern psychology"; in 1879, at the University of Leipzig, he established the first psychological laboratory in the world; in 1881 he inaugurated a scientific journal for the publication of psychological research. His book went into six revised editions and grew in size from one large volume to three; the laboratory prospered, and research students, drawn from near and far, filled the journal with reports of psychological experiments.

Wundt, himself, was tireless. Besides the work of instructing, administering, editing, and directing research, he wrote voluminously. His *Physiological Psychology* will be considered in a moment, but there were also books on other phases of psychology, as well as texts in philosophy, ethics, and logic, to occupy his time. It has been estimated that he published, on the average, more than two pages a day for 68 years; and none of this material is light reading.

In the *Physiological Psychology*, Wundt gives us our first psychological *system*. He tells us what psychology is; he outlines its methods of investigation; he points to its problems; and he classifies the results already obtained. Out of the breadth and depth of his philosophic and scientific training, supplemented with laboratory findings, he brings us the first real handbook of the new science.

A little later, we shall examine, in some detail, a system set forth by one of Wundt's most famous pupils. This system was so close to Wundt's, and so much easier to describe, that we shall not here dwell to any great extent upon the founder's pronouncements. It will be enough to mention a few of the principal characteristics with which he stamped the new science.

First of all, and like many others since the time of Hartley, Wundt was a psychophysical parallelist with respect to the mind-body problem. On the one hand was the physical world, the world of material objects; on the other there was the mental, the world of mind. Psychology was to deal primarily with the latter and could therefore be defined as "the science of immediate experience." By *experience,* Wundt meant such phenomena as sensations, perceptions, feelings, and emotions.

The method to be used by the psychologist, according to Wundt, was *introspection*, a term that was much misused in later days. To Wundt, it meant no more than the *having* of experience. "Having" was equated with "observing." As for the "world out there," it was for him just so much experience or "mental process," and when one *had* it, he had *observed* it.

The problem for psychology was really the problem of what to do about this experience scientifically, and Wundt's answer was threefold: experience was to be *analyzed* into its elements; the elements were in turn to be examined with respect to *the nature of their connections*, one with the other; and, finally, *the laws of their connections* were to be determined.

It should be apparent to the reader that these notions, especially of analysis and association ("connections") are by no means new in the history of our problem. Nevertheless, Wundt brought to them the ordered mind of a man trained in scientific modes of thought and accustomed to careful, rigidly maintained distinctions—in a word, the technique of the physiologist. There is a wide gap between the experienced "idea" of the British empiricist and the sensory or imaginal "process" of Wundtian introspection. For example, the idea of *elephant* or *everything* is a different kind of mental element than the sensation or image of *red* or *C-sharp*, and only the latter would have been acceptable to Wundt as true elements. Analysis of *elephant* (into sensation, image, or both) might be possible—was, indeed, inevitable—with a careful description of experience, but a mental dissection of such a simple unit as *red* could not be made. Wundt proposed to get down to fundamental, irreducible elements before he undertook to show their relation to each other in the fusions and the combinations of everyday mental life.

Significant studies in the physiology of vision, hearing, and the other senses had been carried out already by such men as Helmholtz, Fechner, and Weber (who anticipated some of Fechner's work). These Germans had opened the road to an experimental analysis of the sort that Wundt respected, and it isn't strange that his new text reported many of their methods and data. In addition, however, the *Physiological Psychology* contained material on images, feelings, attention, action, and a wealth of other processes. In fact, there was hardly anything "psychological" that escaped the eye of the founder; and it is little wonder that his textbook set the style for many years to come.

Finally, we return to Wundt's psychophysical parallelism. He believed that for every mental process there was a corresponding, concurrent, physical process. Stimuli of the external world, acting upon sense organs, aroused nervous impulses which, in turn, gave rise to brain activity. With the brain activity came mental activity, but the former did not truly *cause* the latter, nor could the latter cause the former. There were two distinct spheres of activity, one physiological, the other psychological; and "physiological psychology" seemed to Wundt the best way in which to designate the two-fold interest of the new psychology and the intimate relationship between the two fields of research.

We can now begin to see the shape and complexion of 19th century psychology. It was primarily a product of the union of philosophy and physiology. Its subject matter was mind (experience, consciousness), its method was introspective, analytical, and experimental; and its problem was to describe the content or structure of mind in terms of elements and their combinations. In addition, it dealt with questions of mental development and evolution, of cause and effect, of the innate and the acquired; and it had something to say about language, memory, thought, volition, and kindred psychological topics. Its philosophy was predominantly parallelistic and it sought to explain the mind's relation to the body by the use of the methods of science.

Wundt's influence was tremendous. His pupils and his books carried his teachings to far-off parts of the civilized world, arousing a keen interest in the teasing apart of mind with the "brass instruments" of physiology. New laboratories were set up in various universities, new courses of instruction were offered, new psychological journals appeared, and new textbooks were written.

Ultimately, of course, new systems of psychology came into being. Our present task would be much simpler if they had not, but it is the nature of any healthy science to grow and change, to revise its program from time to time. Differences of opinion were bound to arise, even among Wundt's most loyal pupils, as to the subject matter, the methods, and the problems of our science.

A system of psychology is, in a sense, nothing more than a logical framework into which may be fitted the findings of the science. It represents an attempt, usually by one man, to arrange and coordinate the facts of psychology in a simple, understandable fashion. When one man's system or point of view is found acceptable to a number of others who take an active part in spreading its influence, a "school" of psychology is ordinarily the result. Not all systems beget schools, but a school cannot live without a distinct allegiance to a system. When that allegiance is lost, the school disintegrates and the system must be remodeled or supplanted.

This matter of schools is one to which we shall return in later chapters, when we consider the prevailing 'isms of the 1920s and 1930s. They will be better understood, however, in the light of three more historical trends—three other routes to the province of psychology which helped to form the definition of our science.

4

THE STORY
OF THE REFLEX

René Descartes, as the reader of chapter 1 may remember, made a clear distinction between man's *body* and his *mind* (or *soul*), thus setting up a dualism which has stubbornly persisted ever since. Unwittingly, he thereby opened up two main historical routes to psychology as we know it today. The one that we have followed, until now, might be called the *mind* or *mental route*. Except in the case of Hobbes, to whom mind was really *matter*, all the philosophers whom we met were concerned primarily with the origins and content of our mental life. Even Helmholtz, Fecher, and Wundt, in spite of their natural-science training and bias, still focused upon the analysis of the human mind. They simply looked more closely than did their predecessors, finding mental elements (sensations, for example) that were experimentally defined and lawfully related to happenings in the outside world.

The *body route* from Descartes to the present began when this great Frenchman described and mechanism of response in man and the higher animals. In his opinion, as we have seen (p. 3), the sensory nerves were little tubes, with delicate threads that composed their "marrow." When excited by outside agents, the sense organs supposedly acted upon these threads as a bell-ringer might pull upon a bell-rope, opening valves within the brain and permitting *animal spirits* to flow into the tubular motor nerves and thence into the muscles. The muscles themselves, thus swollen by the spirits, produced the appropriate action. The *stimulus*, in this fashion, elicits its *response* and here we have, in essence, the concept of the *reflex*.

It was the middle of the 19th century before natural scientists recognized the basically correct elements of Descartes' thinking— that stimuli cause responses by way of the linked activity of sense organs, sensory nerves, brain (and spinal cord), motor nerves, and muscles or glands. The Cartesian *errors* had to be eliminated before this could come about. For example, it had to be shown that muscles did *not* swell with animal spirits; that the nerves were *not* little tubes, with bell-ropes inside; that the ventricles were less important than the gray matter of the brain. In a word, the whole idea of reflex action, presented so well by Descartes, had to be rediscovered.

The *word* "reflex" is said to have been first used by Jean Astruc, a French doctor, who said that animal spirits from sensory nerves were *reflected* from the spinal cord or brain to motor nerves that happened to be in direct line with them. However, it is generally from the time of Marshall Hall (1790–1857), an English physician-physiologist, that we date the modern use of the term. Although not the "father" of reflex experimentation (there are other contenders for that title), Hall was clearly the "founder." He carried out many studies, chiefly of decapitated animals; he wrote and lectured extensively on the topic; and he attracted the interest of countless others to this field of investigation.

Hall's initial observations were made in 1832, while he was studying circulation in the lungs of a newt. With a friend, a "Mr. Henry Smith," he had removed the head of a triton and cut the "insensible" body into three separate parts. To the great surprise of both observers, when they stimulated the tail "with the point of a probe or forceps," they saw it "move and become contorted into varied forms!" From this and other observations, Hall was led, in 1850, to conclude that the connection between the "irritations" and the movements must involve the action of sensory nerves (he called them *esodic*), the spinal cord (he said the *marrow*), and motor nerves (*exodic*). He referred to the whole physiological-anatomical sequence as the *diastaltic system*, to contrast it with the *peristaltic* function of the stomach and other organs.

As early as 1833, Hall wrote of four different modes of reaction: (1) *voluntary*, originating spontaneously in the brain; (2) *respiratory*, arising in the medulla oblongata (also spontaneously); (3) *involuntary*, caused by directly stimulating the muscles themselves; and (4)) *reflex*, aroused by sense-organ stimulation (as noted above) and reflected from the spinal cord to the appropriate muscles. There is nothing very new in this classification, but it may be worth noting that the voluntary-reflex distinction had been made by Descartes 200 years before, and is still being made today, 140 years later.

After Marshall Hall, studies of reflex action came so fast and from so many directions that one cannot easily hold to the main historical trail. Who came first with this or that important fact or observation, or who influenced whom, cannot always be stated with assurance. One may, however, distinguish between two main approaches to the problem.

First, there were those who thought of the reflex as an observable *stimulus-response connection*—a connection that was sometimes called unlearned, involuntary, or even unconscious. These observers followed the lead of David Hartley, whose associationism and mind-body views were noted in chapter 1. Under the heading of *Automatic Motions*, he had listed a number of commonly observed reactions and the senses on which they seemed to depend. He noted the grasping response of an infant when touched on the palm of the hand; the pupillary constriction of the eye in response to light; the "suction" response of an infant to "taste"; the sneezing response to "smell" (and to strong light); as well as a number of other movements that we class today as reflex.

Biologists, medical men, and others who followed in this tradition, often concerned themselves with making lists of such observable connections, as found in animals and human beings, without concern for their dependence on nervous-system function. This cataloguing of reflexes has, indeed, continued into modern times and will be mentioned later in these pages.

Another, larger group of investigators turned to the *mechanism* of reflex function, rather than the mere relation of two observed events. With the aid of dissecting instruments, compound micro-scopes, and new techniques of tissue staining, nerve stimulation, and recording of response, they sought to tease out the train of activities that started in the sense organs and ended in the action of muscles or glands. They worked almost always with animal subjects, but almost never with normal, intact organisms. They used special "prepara-tions"—animals in which one part of the nervous system was surgically separated from another, as by cutting through the spinal cord or severing the connection between different parts of the brain.

The flowering of such research came in one of the first great books of the 20th century, *The Integrative Action of the Nervous System*, by Charles S. Sherrington (1857–1952), a British physiologist and winner of the Nobel prize. Published in 1906, this book contained most of the basic facts of reflex action, collected by scientists down through the years. These facts were sifted and arranged by Sherrington to clarify the functional elements of the simplest reflex hook-up; to show how different reflex units worked together simultaneously or in sequence; and to establish a physiological concept, that of the *synapse*, of considerable importance.

The reader has already seen what Descartes would have called a reflex (p. 3), and has also heard the views of Marshall Hall (p. 24). He may, then, like to know how Sherrington described it.

The conception of a reflex . . . embraces that of at least three separable structures,—an *effector* organ, e.g., gland cells or muscle cells; a conducting nervous path or *conductor* leading to that organ; and an initiating organ or *receptor* whence the reaction starts. The conductor consists . . . of at least two nerve-cells, one connected with the receptor, the other with the effector. For our purpose the receptor is best included as a part of the nervous system, and so it is convenient to speak of the whole chain of structures—receptor, conductor, and effector—as a reflex-arc.

Sherrington says that this reflex arc, or reflex, is "*the unit reaction in nervous integration*," but he also tells us that a *simple reflex*, of the sort suggested by his description, "is probably a purely abstract conception, because all parts of the nervous system are connected together and no part of it is probably ever capable of reaction without affecting and being affected by various other parts . . . ."

Also of interest, even today, is Sherrington's treatment of reflex *combination*, especially reflex *chaining*—the objective counterpart of the British empiricist's "successive association of ideas." His discussion of the "orderly sequence of movement [which] characterizes the outward behavior of animals" is one that not only displays his full appreciation of the cooperating factors and complex interactions that exist when "one act succeeds another without confusion," but also reveals his desire to understand the normal, coordinated behavior of "unmutilated" animals. Sherrington can never be accused of oversimplifying the problems, restricting the aims, or underestimating the ultimate reach of the sciences to which he contributed so much.

Sherrington usually dealt, however, with operated animals, as did reflex physiologists in general. Especially useful in his researches was the "spinal dog," an animal in which the "fore-dog" was separated from the "hind-dog" by cutting through the spinal cord. If such an animal, upon recovery from the operation, is suitably stimulated on its flank, its hind paw, or its tail, special reflex actions will occur and can be studied in detail, unaffected by influence from the higher centers of the nervous system. The properties of behavior thus observed may be compared with those from other "preparations," in which the spinal cord may not be involved at all, as when conduction is restricted to a section of motor "nerve trunk" leading to an excised muscle—a so-called nerve-muscle preparation.

Throughout many pages of his book, Sherrington amasses evidence to show that nervous conduction through a reflex arc is different from conduction over a comparable length of nerve-trunk tissue. He says, for example, that reflex-arc conduction is slower than that in the nerve trunk; that its threshold of stimulation is more variable in height; that it shows more "after-discharge" when stimulation ends; and that there is less correspondence between the stimulus intensity and that of the response. He traces these and other differences to the existence of a *synapse* or "surface of separation" between each adjacent pair of nerve cells in the reflex arc.

Sherrington's work was of interest to psychologists as well as reflex physiologists. Many students of learning, for example, saw in the synapse a device for switching nervous impulses from one pathway to another in the nervous system—a device that might be useful in explaining adaptive changes in behavior or even new associations of ideas. Then, as earlier (and later), psychologists were trying to account for both mental life and bodily movement in terms of happenings in the nervous system.

A few readers of Sherrington's book recognized that it was concerned with stimulus-response relations that were of interest *in themselves*, regardless of their reference to the nervous system. The organisms that he described were usually laboratory preparations, surgically "insulted" to a greater or less degree; but the measures that he used were measures of *behavior*, in response to special stimulation, and had relevance to more than purely physiological affairs. A useful distinction was made between the *reflex arc*, a receptor-conductor-effector *mechanism*, and the *reflex*, a simple *stimulus-response relation* which might be studied even when no reference was intended to physiological events. The door was thereby opened to a science of behavior that was largely free from physiological concerns (see chapter 13).

Sherrington was well acquainted with the psychology of his day. He knew about the work of Fechner, Wundt, and William James; he cited with approval the teachings of Romanes, Morgan, Thorndike (see chapter 6), and others; and some psychologists (e.g., R.S. Woodworth) came to study in his laboratory. He was greatly concerned with the *voluntary* control of reflex action, which, like others before him, he related to the functions of the brain, "where psychical factors loom large." After years of studying "brainless" organisms, Sherrington ends his account of such researches with the statement that it is "around the cerebrum, its physiological and psychological attributes, that the main interest of biology must ultimately turn."

As if in fulfillment of this prediction, our next historical figure begins his greatest book at the very point where Sherrington left off. Ivan Petrovich Pavlov (1849–1936), in the opening sentence of his *Conditioned Reflexes* (1927), asserts that "the cerebral hemispheres stand out as the crowning achievement in the nervous development of the animal kingdom"; and the next 410 pages may properly be considered as an heroic attempt to clarify those functions of the brain which his British contemporary felt to be so needful of attention.

Like Sherrington, Pavlov was a Nobel prize recipient, in 1904. Like Sherrington, too, his views of nervous-system function were based largely on seen and measured relationships of stimulus to response, and his contributions to the science of behavior are at least as important as any he may have made to his own field of specialization—the workings of the mammalian nervous system.

Unlike Sherrington, however, Pavlov and his pupils worked with animals (dogs) possessed of *intact*, rather than operated, nervous systems; focused on *glandular* response rather than muscular; and, most important, dealt primarily with those reflexes that were *acquired* within an animal's lifetime.

Pavlov's name today is known to every schoolboy, and psychology students all over the world become acquainted with conditioned reflexes early in their education. Rarely do they get, however, the full import of Pavlov's contribution or discover its relation to the systematic thinking of our times. A word or two at this point may therefore help to place this famous Russian in perspective.

Historically, the *experimental* study of the reflex probably began with casual observations of simple muscular contraction in response to the direct stimulation of the muscle itself—e.g., the "involuntary" twitching of a dissected frog's leg when given a slight electric shock. Later on, as Marshall Hall observed in his decapitated newts and snakes, widespread response was observed to stimuli *at a distance* from the effector organ, say on the surface of the skin. By Sherrington's time, as we have seen, living animals were used as subjects, measures of stimulus and response were greatly refined, and all but the highest nervous centers were occasionally involved.

With all of this advance, however, a critical step was still to be taken, for which the times were hardly ripe. Most physiologists were apparently sure that any higher animal, with a normally functioning brain, would defy the procedures of natural science. Something "mental" or "psychic" might enter the picture to distort the lawful cause-effect relations on which a science must depend.

Among the few who dared to question this assumption was Ivan Mikhailovich Sechenov (1829–1905), a Russian physiologist who is sometimes called the father of "reflexology." In 1863, Sechenov wrote a book entitled (in English) *The Reflexes of the Brain*, wherein he expressed the bold opinion that "all acts of conscious or

unconscious life are reflexes"—an opinion which nearly led him into court as "immoral" and "materialistic."

Sechenov's book was popular, it is said, among the Russian "intelligentsia" of the day. However that may, be we know that Pavlov read it, while still in his teens, and that it made a profound and long-lasting impression upon him. It may even have steered him into the field of physiology and, ultimately, the physiology of the brain. Years later, he described it as "an attempt, brilliant and truly extraordinary for the time . . . to picture our subjective world in a purely physiological aspect"; and, on many other occasions, Pavlov acknowledged his debts to Sechenov—not only for his rejection of mind-body dualism and the study of "the complete and undivided [animal organism], instead of a vague half," but especially for his belief in the dependence of an organism upon its environment—a belief that was well reflected in Pavlov's stress upon the *stimulus* control of behavior.

In spite of Sechenov's effect upon his thinking, when Pavlov first observed the glandular secretion in a hungry dog to stimuli that had apparently *acquired* their power to excite, he did not immediately conclude that he had a physiological matter to consider. When he found that salivation could be evoked by simply presenting the animal with its empty food plate, he spoke of this new stimulus-response connection as a "psychic" reflex. It wasn't long, however, before he dropped the mental reference and decided to treat the phenomenon as he would have treated any other reflex function.[1]

Pavlov was not (and *knew* he was not) the first to note the basic phenomenon of conditioning. Claude Bernard, the father of experimental physiology, had reported, in 1872, identical observations, except that they were made of horses, rather than dogs; Robert Whytt, a Scot, had said as long ago as 1763 that "the sight, or even the recalled *idea* of grateful food, causes an uncommon flow of spittle into the mouth of a hungry person . . . "; and there were surely many others.

---

[1] This led to a heated debate with A. T. Snarsky, one of Pavlov's colleagues, who had used *dilute acid* as a basis for conditioning salivary flow, just as Pavlov had used food. Snarsky insisted on a "psychological" explanation of his findings and, after a lengthy confrontation with his senior, had to leave the laboratory.

But it was Pavlov who grasped the significance of what he had seen and undertook to reproduce what nature had achieved when she "taught" a dog to salivate in response to food-at-a-distance or on being presented with his empty food dish. By sounding a bell, for example, just before giving food to a hungry dog, and doing this on numerous occasions; by testing the animal every so often with the sound of the bell alone (measuring the *amount* of salivary flow and the *time* it took to begin); and by keeping other factors constant in the experimental situation, Pavlov was able to set up the classic relation of stimulus to response which the world now calls "conditioned reflex"

For nearly 40 years after his pioneer investigations, this new province was explored by Pavlov and his pupils. The early, rather primitive methods of stimulating and recording were improved and extended. Financial aid was secured and a research center was developed. Medical students and others came to work in Pavlov's laboratory and under Pavlov's guidance, in an atmosphere of intimacy, cooperation, industry, and high purpose. Countless new facts were collected and, most importantly, a system of behavior was gradually developed—a system that, for Pavlov, was meant to describe the functions of the brain. In brief, the concept of the reflex underwent a great expansion the like of which Descartes could never have imagined.

The principle of conditioning was only one of those included within the Pavlovian scheme. As early as 1904, in his Nobel prize address at Stockholm, Pavlov talked about the *extinction* of an already-conditioned reflex by presenting the "conditioned stimulus" (e.g., food-at-a-distance) without the "reinforcing stimulus" (the food-in-the-mouth) with which it had earlier been paired. "If the dog is repeatedly stimulated with the sight of objects inducing a salivary secretion from a distance, the reaction of the salivary glands becomes weaker and weaker and finally drops to zero."[2]

Another important element of this Pavlovian structure was the principle of *generalization*, the objective equivalent of the associationist's "law of similarity" and a first approximation to the basic

---

[2] This quotation is taken from Michael Kaplan's *Essential Works of Pavlov* (Bantam Books, 1966), pp. 53–4.

concerns of men like Helmholtz and Fechner. The classic experiment is one in which Pavlov conditioned a dog to salivate in response to a 1000-cycle tone. When the response was well-established, he tested the animal's reaction to a number of other tones, and found them all effective, although in different degrees. Tones that were near in frequency to the conditioned stimulus elicited the greatest amount of salivation; those that were furthest away elicited the least. A "gradient" of stimulus generalization was apparent.

An additional principle, based on the previous three, was that of stimulus *discrimination*, a principle that brings us even closer to the interests of sensory physiology. When there was continued reinforcement of the above mentioned conditioned reflex to the 1000-cycle, tone, but *non-reinforcement* (i.e., *extinction*) of the generalizing reflexes, the experimental animal ultimately came to respond *only* when the conditioned stimulus was presented. The generalizing stimuli finally lost their power, through extinction, to elicit salivary flow. A discrimination had been made between the conditioned stimulus and the other tones along the frequency scale.

Pavlov explained these behavioral facts and certain others (e.g., those of sleep, hypnosis, time discrimination, and "neurosis") in terms of physiological *excitations, inhibitions*, and *irradiations* within the cerebral hemispheres. In such hypothesizing, he makes his closest contact with the teachings of Sechenov, Sherrington, and others, but this was not his greatest contribution to the story of the reflex for students of psychology. More important for them, by far, were the objective facts and the laws that were based upon them.

In addition to all this, Pavlov gave, us the beginnings of a *system* of behavior. He showed us, for example, how conditioning was related to extinction, how conditioning *and* extinction exhibited generalization, and how all of these were included within discrimination. Facts were not considered apart from other facts, but were brought together within an integrated whole, which is sometimes called a "theory." Only with the aid of such integrations, can students master the details of a science, contribute meaningfully to its structure, or apply its findings broadly to practical spheres of life.

Other effects of Pavlov on our science will be described in later chapters of this book. Before we leave the present one, however, something should be said about another Russian, often spoken of as

Pavlov's rival. Vladimir Mikhailovich Bekhterev (1857–1927) was a neurologist and psychiatrist, whose interests and activities ranged through many fields, from anatomy to education, and whose early training included time with Wundt, at Leipzig, and with Charcot, the famous neurologist, in Paris. Influenced by Sechenov's teachings and well-acquainted with Pavlov's work, he sought to turn the study of "association-reflexes" (his term) into more practical channels. Arguing that the salivary reflex was "inapplicable to man" and that Pavlov's motor-conditioning attempts were insufficiently exact, Bekhterev and his pupils established several "association-motor reflexes" in dogs and human subjects. Respiration and foot withdrawal served as basic reflexes in the animal studies, while foot and hand (or finger) withdrawal served for the human beings.

Detailed accounts of his procedure as it gradually developed are difficult to find, even in Bekhterev's own writings. His "fundamental" stimulus was an electric shock, corresponding to the food in Pavlov's studies. Each shock was paired with a tone or other neutral stimulus. After a number of pairings, the tone alone was given, to see if the withdrawal or other motor response had become "associated" with the neutral stimulus. It appears that, if the response occurred on any such test occasion, the tone was simply repeated *without* the shock for another trial, and this was done again and again as long as the subject responded. In other words, the subject could avoid the tone-shock combinations by responding to the tone alone whenever it was given. Without this possibility, the association reflex was difficult to establish.[3]

Today it may be argued that Bekhterev, unknowingly, suggested limits to the conditioned-reflex principle, either Pavlov's or his own—that his attempt to improve upon one concept simply showed the need for another—one that we shall approach in chapter 5. In a sense, he brought the *physiological* story of the reflex to its end; his studies had their greatest effect on *psychological* method, as Pavlov's had on psychological theory—facts that will become apparent as we move along.

---

[3] The technique here described was used by Watson (chapter 9) with a hand-withdrawal response in 1916 and is based upon the one that Bekhterev employed.

5

VOLUNTARY BEHAVIOR
AND ITS CONTROL

By 1833, when Marshall Hall distinguished between *reflex* and several other functions, especially the *voluntary*, he was not the first to come up with this distinction. Descartes had recognized the difference between responses evoked by *stimuli* and those which happened at the behest of man's *soul*. He even described, as the reader knows, the means by which the soul might overrule a reflex action by moving the pineal gland, thus diverting animal spirits from their accustomed channels. Thomas Hobbes was another who talked about *voluntary motion*, contrasting it with *vital motion*, and finding it basic to what he called *endeavour* (pp. 6–7), David Hartley, in 1749, made a similar distinction, between *automatic* movements (p. 25), arising from sense-organ stimulation, and *voluntary* ones, which had their origin in *ideas*. And these are but a few of the greats within psychology's past to talk about this matter.

We have seen how the study of the reflex, in an experimental setting, went forward at a rapid pace in the wake of Marshall Hall's investigations. Voluntary acts, however, did not so readily bow to scientific rule. Any behavior that was seemingly unrelated to any obvious physical cause was always a source of worry to biologists and other natural-science workers. Often it was dropped, like an unwanted child, at the doorstep of the science having most to do with "mental" causes—psychology, that is. Voluntary behavior was, for some, by definition, outside the boundaries of prediction and control. What better could be done about it than let psychologists describe the way it *felt* when it occurred?

Attempts, indeed, were often made, in the days of Wundt and later, to apply the method of introspection to this problem, but the principal advance in treating voluntary action seems to have depended on two important factors: (1) its linkage with another age-old concept, that of *hedonism* (from the Greek, *hedone*, meaning "pleasure") and (2) the observational study of *trial-and-error* behavior. Let us take these matters up in order.

The doctrine that pleasure or pain determines human conduct has been expressed in various ways and at many times since the beginnings of recorded history. It has played a part in the thinking of philosophers in particular, from the days of Aristippus (c. 435–356 B. C.) and Epicurus (341–270 B. C.) down to the present. It appeared in the writings of John Locke, of Thomas Hobbes, of David Hume, and other associationists; and it was a very important feature of the utilitarian philosophy ("the greatest good to the greatest number") of Jeremy Bentham (1748–1832), who expressed his central position in the following way:

Nature has placed mankind under thy governance of two sovereign masters, pain and pleasure. It is for them alone to point out what we ought to do, as well as to determine what we shall do. On the one hand the standard of right and wrong, on the other the chain of causes and effects, are fastened to their throne. They govern us in all we do, in all we say, in all we think: every effort we can make to throw off their subjection will serve but to demonstrate and confirm it.[1]

One of the first to bring together the notions of hedonism and volition in a way to suggest the teachings of modern times, was Alexander Bain (1818–1903). Born a poor boy in Scotland, the son of an Aberdeen weaver, Bain managed, by his own efforts, to get a college education, to teach and write in a number of fields

[1] Jeremy Bentham, *An Introduction to the Principles of Morals and Legislation*, 1879.

(mathematics, logic, philosophy, English), and to become Great Britain's first psychologist, in everything but formal title. Through his writings, he made contact with John Stuart Mill (a strong *utilitarian* in his youth) with whom he established frendship and a working relation for several years. He wrote two successful text-books—*The Senses and the Intellect* (1855) and *The Emotions and the Will* (1859)—and he founded the first psychological journal, *Mind*, five years before Wundt launched his Leipzig journal, *Philosophische Studien*. Even more than Wundt's, Bain's writings have the feel of psychology as it is taught today.

One of the problems that Bain attempted to solve was how the *will* develops in animals or human beings. His fairly complicated answer to this question is of interest to us here. First, he says, there are *spontaneous movements*—movements unlike reflex actions, which occur in a diffuse or random fashion as a result of the natural function of the nervous system. Some of these movements, by lucky chance, produce a desirable state of affairs, accompanied by conscious pleasure[2] which becomes associated with the movement that brought it on. Whenever the same external conditions occur in the future, the memory of the pleasure sets off the movement again. Frequent repetition strengthens this association between idea and movement until voluntary behavior is established.

In the case of pain-producing movements, a similar argument holds. Here is how Bain describes the way in which an animal might learn to escape from a confining situation by making a certain response: "The repeated connection between the feeling [of displeasure through confinement] and this one movement (at first accidentally stumbled upon) would end in a firm association between the two; there would be no more fumbling and uncertainty; the random tentatives, arising through spontaneity and the spasmodic writhings of pain, would give place to the one selected and appropriate movement and we should have a full-grown volition adapted to the case."[3]

---

[2] "States of Pleasure," says Bain, "are connected with an increase, states of Pain with an abatement of some or all of the Vital functions."

[3] Alexander Bain, *The Emotions and the Will* (4th ed.), 1899. pp. 322 ff.

Some of Bain's thinking about the effects of pleasure and pain on
nonreflex behavior was shared with, even anticipated by, Herbert
Spencer (1820–1903), the English philosopher, "evolutionary associationist," and theorist-at-large.[4] A sample of Spencer's thinking,
from the second edition of his *Principles of Psychology* (1870), will
show how close the two men were. Spencer is discussing the relation
of *concentrated* to *diffuse* discharge of nervous energy, upon which
depends the *special* and *general* excitement in related muscles.

Suppose now, that in putting out its head to seize prey, a creature
has repeatedly failed. Suppose that along with the group of motor
actions approximately adapted to seize prey at this distance, the
diffused discharge is, on some occasion, so distributed . . . as to
cause a slight forward movement of the body. Success will occur
instead of failure; and after success will immediately come certain
pleasurable sensations with an accompanying large draught of
nervous energy towards the organs employed in eating, etc. That is
to say, the lines of nervous communication through which the
diffused discharge happened in this way to pass, have opened up a
new way to certain wide chanels of escape; and . . . rendered more
permeable than before. On recurrence of the circumstances, these
. . . movements that were followed by success are likely to be
repeated: what was at first an accidental combination of motions
will now be a combination having considerable probability . . . . The
tendency for the diffused discharge to follow these lines will
obviously be greater than before; and the probability of a success-
fully modified action will therefore be greater than before. Every
repetition . . . will increase the probability of subsequent repetitions
. . . .[5]

In these teachings of Bain and Spencer, a pattern emerges. First,
there is the idea of *spontaneous* or *accidental movement*, occurring
under conditions of hunger or confinement. Secondly, this movement results in a form of *gratification* or *relief*, as through removal

---

[4] A prolific theorizer in biological and social science, Spencer argued that
mental and physical associations acquired in one generation might beget a
tendency for similar associations in the next. This view reflects his study of
Lamarck, whose work he read before Charles Darwin's. Spencer is said to have
coined the term, *survival of the fittest*.

[5] Herbert Spencer, *Principles of Psychology*, 1870.

of hunger or escape from confinement. Thirdly, this gratification or relief, with its associated *pleasure*, seems to *strengthen the movement* in its connection with the prevailing circumstances, making it more likely to occur on later occasions. Finally, this movement belongs to the class called *voluntary*, rather than reflex.

The examples cited by Spencer and Bain in connection with their theories may have been suggested to them by actual behaviors that they witnessed in situations similar to those described. Their arguments remain, however, at a pretty abstract level, and could profit from objective observational support. Fortunately, this was soon provided for them, and their thinking was extended by another Britisher, who brought their notions one shade closer to experimental test.

C. Lloyd Morgan (1852–1936), a post-Darwinian teacher of zoology, geology, psychology, and evolutionary theory, is best known today as an early *comparative psychologist*, interested in the animal mind as compared with that of human beings, but unwilling to engage in extravagant "humanizing of the brute" (see chapter 6). His contribution to the present theme can best be illustrated by a classic quotation from his first important book, *Animal Life and Intelligence* (1890–91).

Morgan is talking about the accomplishments of Tony, his pet terrier:

The way in which my dog learnt to lift the latch of the garden gate and thus let himself out was in this wise. The iron gate is held to by a latch, but swings open by its own weight if the latch be lifted. Whenever he wanted to go out the fox terrier raised the latch with the back of his head, and thus released the gate, which swung open. Now the question in any such case is: How did he learn the trick? In this particular case the question can be answered, because he was carefully watched. When he was put outside the door, he naturally wanted to get out into the road, where there was much to tempt him—the chance of a run, other dogs to sniff at, possibly cats to be worried. He gazed eagerly out through the railings on the low parapet wall ... ; and in due time chanced to gaze out under the latch, lifting it with his head. He withdrew his head and looked out elsewhere, but the gate had swung open. Here was a fortunate occurrence arising out of the natural tendencies of a dog. But the association between looking out just there and the open gate with a free passage into the road is somewhat indirect. The coalescence of mental processes in a conscious situation effective for the guidance of behavior did not spring into being at once. Only after some ten or twelve experiences, in each of which the exit was more rapidly made, with less gazing out at wrong places, had the fox terrier learnt to go straight and without hesitation to the right spot. *In this case the lifting of the latch was unquestionably hit upon by accident, and the trick was only rendered habitual by repeated association in the same situation of the chance act and happy escape.* Once firmly established, however, the behaviour remained constant throughout the remainder of the dog's life, some five or six years.[6]

In this example of trial-and-error learning, a touch of homely realism is given to the Spencer-Bain pronouncements, in a description that was very objective for the times. Morgan was unusually sensitive to the requirements of good scientific reporting. Yet even this account, from the point of view of later critics, left something still to be desired. There were those who wondered, for example, how he could have known that the "guidance" of his pet's behavior was done by a "coalescence of mental processes in a conscious situation."

Morgan's observation was comparable to Pavlov's when the latter first saw the "psychic secretion" of saliva in one of his dogs. It went somewhat further, however, in its inclusion of an actual change in behavior with successive "trials." It should the more readily have suggested to Morgan the refinements of a laboratory setting. Science often moves by tiny steps, however, and it was left for other workers to make the next advance—especially to E. L. Thorndike.

Edward Lee Thorndike (1874–1949), psychologist, educator, and the first important American to be considered in these pages, became acquainted with our science at Connecticut Wesleyan University. It was there that he sampled the writings of William James (see chapter 8) and decided to go to Harvard for two more years of study. In the course of his work at Harvard, his curiosity led him to experiments on "mind-reading" (in which he rewarded children with bits of candy for accurate guesses) and maze-learning

[6] C. Lloyd Morgan, *Animal Life and Intelligence*.

(with chicks, in James's cellar). The mind-reading study met with objections,[7] but the learning study was successful, and Thorndike took two of his best performers with him to Columbia in 1897, along with an interest in animal intelligence and its measurement.

At Columbia, under James McKeen Cattell[8] (1860–1944), who had brought him there with a fellowship, this interest quickly ripened into laboratory research. Space for working was obtained, crude apparatus was constructed, and *experiments* were undertaken in the sphere of problem solving, with cats and dogs as the principal subjects. Before the end of 1898, a monograph was published on *Animal Intelligence*,[9] in which the new procedure was described, "time-curves" of learning were presented, current conceptions (e.g., Lloyd Morgan's) of the animal mind were questioned, and a new explanation of trial-and-error learning was suggested.

Thorndike's work, like Pavlov's, is commonly described to students in beginners' classes, and the reader of these lines may find nothing new in what has just been said. He may already know that most of Thorndike's studies used hungry cats as subjects; that these animals were placed in "puzzle boxes," crate-like structures, from which they could escape, and get to food, only by lifting a latch, depressing a pedal, or operating some other release device in a carefully specified fashion; that Thorndike measured the time required for each cat to escape from its box in a regular series of "trials"; and that the animals typically reduced this time in a more

[7] "The children," said Thorndike, "enjoyed the experiments, but the authorities in control of the institution would not permit me to continue."

[8] Cattell, a pioneer in American psychology, had studied under Wundt, but was more interested in individual differences than in the typical, adult, normal, human mind. He founded a laboratory at Pennsylvania, where he taught from 1888 to 1891, and at Columbia, to which he came in the latter year. His interests included reaction-time experimentation, mental tests and measurements, the establishment of psychology as a science, and the furtherance of American science in general. He was the first "professor of psychology" in the United States, and Thorndike was one of the first of a long list of doctoral candidates whose researches he sponsored at Columbia.

[9] The full title was *Animal Intelligence: An Experimental Study of the Associative Processes in Animals*. Psychol. Rev., Monogr. Suppl., 1898, 2, No. 8.

or less gradual manner, as the eliminated useless movements and got to "the point" more directly. The reader may even have seen examples of Thorndike's *learning curves*, the first of their kind, in which time-to-escape (in seconds) is plotted against the number of successive opportunities, until the act "is done precisely and at will." And, finally, he has probably heard about Thorndike's famous principle of learning—the so-called *Law of Effect*. Yet he may never have sensed the full importance of this man.

Partly because Thorndike's experiments are so simple, partly because his later studies are given less attention, and partly, perhaps, because he was not a "school" man (see chapter 9), Thorndike is seldom seen as a real transition figure in the history of psychology. He is not perceived as one who stands between the old associationism and modern *reinforcement* theory, between the speculations of a Spencer or a Bain on *adaptation* or *volition* and the systematic treatment of *operant* behavior, or between the field observations of Lloyd Morgan and the elaborate techniques of the modern laboratory. Yet this, in fact, is where he stood.

Consider the Law of Effect, for which he is most famous. Its earliest expression, in 1898, is definitely associationistic, with statements that closely resemble those of Alexander Bain. Thorndike tells us that his aim is to explain "the nature of the process of association in the animal mind." He sees this process as displayed in, and as directing, the animal's acts. The association finally proposed, in accounting for the actions of his cats and other subjects, is an association between the "sense impression" of the problem situation (together with "the feeling of discomfort" due to hunger and confinement) and the "impulse"—the conscious accompaniment of the final adaptive response. This association is achieved because of its successful outcome.

Thorndike finds no need to postulate any other mental elements than those of sense impressions and impulses. ("The possibility is that animals may have no images or memories, no ideas to associate.") In this he moved away from Bain and others, even from Lloyd Morgan, and raised the hackles of many a post-Darwinian exponent of animal ideation. In one provocative sentence, indeed, he says that the associations formed in his experiments "mean simply the connection of a certain act with a certain situation and resultant pleasure .... Except for the puzzling status of "pleasure," this sounds like *stimulus-response* psychology. (We can begin to see why both Sherrington and Pavlov mentioned "Thorndyke" [sic] with approval, why Woodworth[10] later treated him as an "early behaviorist" (see chapter 9), and, especially, why Thorndike spoke of himself as a *connectionist*.)

The Law of Effect was formally stated in 1911, in the book that resulted from Thorndike's doctoral monograph. It goes as follows:

> Of several responses made to the same situation, those which are accompanied or closely followed by satisfaction to the animal will, other things being equal, be more firmly connected with the situation, so that, when it recurs, they will be more likely to recur; those which are accompanied or closely followed by discomfort to the animal will, other things being equal, have their connections with that situation weakened, so that, when it recurs, they will be less likely to occur. The greater the satisfaction or discomfort, the greater the strengthening or weakening of the bond.[11]

In this statement of his principle, Thorndike moved still further away from subjectivity. *Pleasure* and *pain* are replaced by *satisfaction* and *discomfort*; and, to keep his readers from concluding that these terms, too, are mentalistic, he goes on to say: "By a satisfying state of affairs is meant one which the animal does nothing to avoid, often doing such things as attain and preserve it. By a discomforting or annoying state of affairs is meant one which the animal commonly avoids and abandons." This is Thorndike's closest approximation to what the present reader may recognize as the principle of *operant conditioning* (to which we shall return in chapter 12).

A second law was added in the 1911 book—a law that also had its forerunners in association theory, and one that had been implied in his early monograph: "Any response to a situation will, other things being equal, be more strongly connected with the situation in proportion to the number of times it has been connected with that situation and to the average vigor and duration of the connection."

[10] R. S. Woodworth, *Contemporary Schools of Psychology*, 1931.

[11] E. L. Thorndike, *Animal Intelligence*. New York: Macmillan, 1911.

This was Thorndike's *Law of Exercise*. Its antecedents can be found in the writings of Thomas Brown (1778–1820), James Mill and John Stuart Mill, and other associationists, including Herbert Spencer. It is a "law," however, that Thorndike was later to rescind, when he found, in further studies, that repetition of a connection was ineffective *unless* the connection was followed by a "satisfying state of affairs."

In the period between 1898 and 1911, Thorndike followed up his studies of cats, dogs, and chicks with related experiments on monkeys; he accepted a post at Columbia's Teachers College, after a year at Western Reserve; he assisted Professor Cattell, his mentor, in editing *Science* and the *Popular Science Monthly*—a sideline that he dropped at the advice of Jacques Loeb (see chapter 6); he wrote his first book on *Education Psychology* (1903) and a text on *The Elements of Psychology* (1905); and he made numerous other contibutions. Thorndike was an active man.

At Teachers College, he turned to the problem of human learning, classroom procedure, intelligence testing, educational measurement, dictionary making, and other matters, but he never lost sight of his basic law of effect and, from time to time, he added others as his researches seemed to dictate. Two of these deserve mention as rough parallels, in the field of voluntary behavior, of Pavlovian principles, and as precursors of present-day teachings of *reinforcement theorists* (chapter 12).

The *Law of Assimilation* or *Response by Analogy*: "To any new situation man responds as he would to some situation like it, or like some element of it," approaches Pavlov's *generalization* (pp. 31–32). In a Thorndikian example, one who has already learned to respond to the stimulus complex, *abcdelmnop,* will also respond in the same way when presented with *abcdefghi,* on the basis of the common elements, *abcde,* in the old and new situations. This comes even closer to what has been described more recently by Skinner[12] as a generalization between composite stimuli that differ only in their membership.

The *Law of Associative Shifting*, as treated in 1913, was based on the *Law of Analogy*: "Starting with response X made to *abcde* we may successively drop certain elements and add others, until the

---

[12] B. F. Skinner, *The Behavior of Organisms*. New York: Appleton-Century-Crofts, 1938, pp. 171–172.

response is bound to *fghij*, to which perhaps it could never otherwise have been connected." This formulation, reflected today in the procedures of *programmed instruction*, was accompanied by an example from animal training. A bit of fish is dangled above a cat while the trainer says, "Stand up!" With enough such pairings, the animal comes to raise itself upon command, without the presence of the lure.

By means of this stimulus shifting, says Thorndike, we may "get any response of which a learner is capable associated with any situation to which he is sensitive." Thorndike recognizes that this "law" suggests *conditioning*, but does not identify it fully with Pavlov's famous principle. By 1931, in fact, he is able to enumerate, in his *Fundamentals of Learning*, 12 differences between "C-R phenomena and ordinary learning"–that is, between conditioning and associative shifting. In this, he comes nearer to modern teaching–more specifically, to the notion of "discriminative operant," which we shall treat, in chapter 12, as voluntary (operant) behavior which has been brought under stimulus control.

Thorndike's "laws," like the stimuli in associative shifting, were added and subtracted from time to time, with little concern for scientific system. He was led by his data to their formulation, and he dropped them for similar reasons; he had no vested interests in them–except, perhaps, for the law of effect. In other words, he was a man of fresh approaches and penetrating insights, but he was not a *theorist*, in the usual sense of the term. By his own confession, he never promoted a cause or "carried out a career," but always responded to "demands from outside"–of which there were many and to which he responded well.

E. L. Thorndike was not a conventional "psychologist," either in the focus of his interests or the development of his skills. He never taught a standard course or worked within a standard department; he says that he was weak in machinery and physical instruments, clumsy with animals,[13] and helpless when calculus was necessary. He would never get a Ph. D. today! But he was a very important man and his name will long be with us.

---

[13] The story is told that, while looking for an errant cat in the attic of Schermerhorn Hall at Columbia, where he did his early researches, Thorndike (a large man) fell between the rafters of an uncovered space and was left, with legs dangling into the occupied classroom below, until help was summoned.

6

THE ANIMAL
AND ITS MIND

Another route to the 20th-century definition of psychology remains to be explored, and again we take as a starting point the teachings of Descartes. Once more we note his dualism of body and mind, or soul, but now we emphasize his claim that man alone possesses both. Animals, he said, are simply bodies, *automata*, machines, devoid of consciousness and reason, their "sensations" being only nervous movements.

This belief may have ennobled man, avoided Church disfavor, and encouraged the practice of vivisection, but, with rare exceptions, it does not relfect the thinking of earlier, or later, days. From time immemorial, every man's feeling about the inner life of animals, especially those he brought within his home, was one of greater generosity and kinship than was Descartes'. And who, today, can observe the twitching legs and muffled bark of a sleeping dog without attributing a private life to the animal which is similar to our own?

For two centuries after Descartes, and in spite of the great philosopher's teachings, a mind of one sort or another was commonly assigned to animals, and usually localized within the brain (where Descartes himself had effectually placed it for *homo sapiens*); but it was not until Charles Darwin (1809–1822) that we find the bold assertion that "there is no fundamental difference between man and the higher mammals in their mental faculties." The difference that *can* be shown to exist, says he, is "of degree and not of kind."[1]

In the behavior of many higher animals, either as he observed it or, more often, as it was reported to him, Darwin found much reason to believe in *mental evolution* and to accept the existence of rudimentary human "faculties" among many subhuman forms. Since animals possess the same senses as man, says he, they have the same "intuitions"; and he notes that they also have instincts in common (e.g., self-preservation, sexual love, and maternal love). He asserts that mammals other than man are able to feel pleasure and pain, to experience happiness and misery, and to be moved by terror; that they may show suspicion, even deceit, and fidelity; and that they give evidence of courage, love, grief, jealousy, emulation, shame, pride, magnanimity, love of approbation, and a dislike for being laughed at.

Darwin bestowed a mental life upon man's cousins with a very open hand, without the self-critical zeal that marked his biological endeavors; but his general position on the evolution of behavior as well as organic structure was ultimately to have a profound effect upon the definition of our science. In his work originated a *comparative* psychology that stressed both differences and similarities between the species, and from which stemmed our present-day reliance upon animal studies in understanding basic human action.

If Charles Darwin was lavish in dispensing human mental faculties among subhuman species, some of his strongest supporters were equally or more so. One of these was George John Romanes (1848–1894). Canadian-born, Cambridge-trained, and converted from the Church to Darwinism, this man has often been cited for his over-generosity in ascribing mind to lower forms. Some of his assertions were, indeed, open to dispute (e.g., he said that the moth flies to the candle because of "curiosity"), and some of the anecdotes to which he lent belief could better be described as fables. But, on the other hand, he made some positive contributions.

[1] Charles Darwin, *The Descent of Man*, 1871, Chapter IV.

In his *Animal Intelligence* (1882), he drew together much behavioral data, from many species, with the aim of showing that animals possess in varying degrees the mental life of man. In this book, he set the pattern for comparative psychology texts for many years to come. Secondly, he argued that mental life in any animal, or in any other *human being*, cannot be directly observed, but can only be *inferred*. Just as we conceive of the mind of God through analogy with our own (*anthropomorphism*, so-called), we use a kind of "inverted anthropomorphism," says Romanes, in constructing the *animal* mind. Our knowledge of the mind in animals or human beings is based, therefore, on its "embassadors"—the bodily movements, the responses of the organism.

Not all behavior, however, suggests the existence of mental life—not all of it shows "intentional choice," the trademark of the mental. We may be deceived, says he, by the purposive appearance of many *reflex* actions, which are *non*mental, inherited, and particular responses to specific situations. A better criterion of mind or consciousness would therefore be: "Does the organism learn to make new adjustments, or to modify old ones, in accordance with the results of its own individual experience?" If it can, it possesses a mind.

Romanes goes one step further. If animals show that they can learn, and are therefore conscious, any additional inference of special mental states will depend upon how closely their behavior resembles ours. We can assume that actions of affection, jealousy, and so forth, in a dog or monkey indicate states of mind very much like our own; but when we infer anger in a bee from outward signs, we do so with less assurance. As we go down through the animal kingdom, says Romanes, our analogy from human to brute psychology weakens.

In his own inferring of mental life in animals, Romanes attempted to be careful, and it appears that he was more so than some other post-Darwinians. He was unwilling, for example, to credit animals, even higher animals, with abstract reasoning or "notional ideas," which he said belonged to man alone. Also, with respect to the reports that he included within his *Animal Intelligence,* he tells us that he accepted facts only on "the authority of some name." He says he was especially alert to possible error in the case of unknown reporters, keeping a record of their "facts" for later confirmation by independent observers.

History has judged, however, that Romanes' precautions were not enough—that a great deal of purely anecdotal matter crept into his work. As a later writer[2] noted, the anecdotal method has its problems. The person who makes the report is often untrained in separating what he actually sees from what he infers; he may be unacquainted with the habits of the species or with the individual history of the animal concerned; he may have a personal affection for his subject and wish to show off its superior intelligence; or he may simply have succumbed to the common desire to tell a good story.

C. Lloyd Morgan, whose observations of his dog, Tony, were described in chapter 5, was one of the first to recognize these dangers and to try to halt the spread of excessive anecdotalism and anthropomorphic tendencies. It was he, perhaps more than any other, who led serious students of animal behavior out of the haze of sentiment and dramatic instance into the clear air of field experiment and sober evaluation, showing them the road to behavioral science.

Like Romanes, Morgan believed in mental, as well as physical, evolution, and he argued that one can never know, directly, any mind besides his own—that all others must be inferred solely from certain conduct. An intelligent clock, he says, would have to infer the minds of other clocks from their "behavior"—the movement of the hands upon the dial. (If the clock was able to look inside the others, the inference might be better, through knowledge of the structure, but it would still be inference.)

In this connection, Morgan writes that the introspective analysis of one's own mind is basic to an understanding of the animal mind, or that of other human beings. "Objective induction," he says, must follow "subjective induction" and must depend upon it. He adds that many good observers of animal behavior display much less skill

[2] Margaret Floy Washburn, *The Animal Mind*, 1926.

is dealing with the animal mind, simply through lack of adequate psychological training.

The fact that we begin with our own subjective world, however, does not mean that we should reason from it to another organism's loosely. On this point, Morgan is emphatic and gives us a rule to follow: "In no case may we interpret an action as the outcome of the exercise of a higher physical faculty if it can be interpreted as the outcome of one which stands lower in the psychological scale."

This principle of interpretation, widely known today as "Lloyd Morgan's canon," was criticized by some as ungenerous to the animal, lacking in simplicity, even illogical. Morgan replies that (1) over-generosity in assigning mental faculties may be socially desirable with respect to other human beings, but in the case of animals we shouldn't begin by assuming that which is still to be proved; (2) "the simplicity of an explanation is no necessary criterion of its truth"; and (3) a frank and unrestrained inference of complex mental activities in an animal, based upon a knowledge of our own, is inconsistent with our belief in (a) the evolution of organic structure from simple to complex, and (b) the parallelism that exists between the physical and the mental.

Morgan gives us various examples to illustrate the application of his rule. One of these, already familiar to the reader (see pp. 39–40), is that of Tony, the dog that learned to lift the latch of the garden gate. According to Morgan, his pet's behavior demonstrated a simple *association* (his word is *coalescence*) of conscious processes; but he denies that the dog had "any conception of the relation of means employed to the end attained." The animal had intelligence, but not reason; and Morgan suggests that animals in general "do not think the therefore."

Within the province of psychology, since the days of Helmholtz, Fechner, and Wundt, the German tongue has often been heard. A good example, in the present context, is the case of Jacques Loeb (1859–1924). Loeb was born in the Rhineland, trained at the University of Strassburg (then in Germany), and spent the last 33 years of his life in teaching and research in the United States. He was a zoologist and physiologist, whose psychological claim to fame rests mainly on his quantitative studies and mechanistic theory of animal behavior.[3]

Unlike Darwin, Romanes, and Morgan, Loeb found little reason to infer an animal mind of any sort. His position, briefly stated, was that all the "voluntary and instinctive actions of animals," including those of man himself, were "determined by internal or external forces," and could be treated by the methods of physical science. Any other way of explaining such actions were, in his opinion, largely "verbalistic" in character.

"What the metaphysician calls consciousness," Loeb argued, depends upon the mechanism of *associative memory*, a mechanism of the brain whereby a stimulus produces, not just its own natural and direct effect, but also the effects of some other stimulus that may have been earlier paired with it in time. (It comes, therefore, as no surprise when Loeb goes on to say that Pavlov is the only one to have yet developed a method for the analysis of this mechanism.)

This capacity to learn, which implies associative memory, is present in most mammals—"the dog which comes when its name is called, which runs away from the whip, which welcomes its master joyfully"; in birds—"the parrot learns to talk, the dove finds its way home"; in some frogs and, perhaps, some fishes; but is very difficult to demonstrate with animals that are lower in the evolutionary scale. All of which leads Loeb to conclude: "The statements of enthusiasts who discover consciousness and resemblance to man on every side should not be too readily accepted."[4]

Loeb's position was to reach its flower later, in the teachings of John Watson, the *behaviorist*, whose work we shall take up in chapter 9. But most psychologists of his day did not agree that all

[3] Loeb was also the scientific idol of many young turks in this country, during the first half of this century. This was due in part to the fact that Sinclair Lewis, in his popular novel, *Arrowsmith* (1925), used him as a model for *Max Gottlieb*, an inspiring, but demanding and uncompromising, laboratory genius.

[4] Jacques Loeb, *Comparative Physiology of the Brain and Comparative Psychology, 1900* (published in German in 1899). A similar argument is made in Loeb's *Forced Movements, Tropisms, and Animal Conduct* (1918), a book that was required reading for students of animal behavior in the 1920s and the 1930s.

reference to the animal's consciousness or mental life was useless. More popular, by far, were the opinions of Herbert Spencer Jennings (1868–1947), a zoologist at Johns Hopkins University and an authority on the behavior of lower animal forms—including that of one-celled animals such as *Paramecium* and *Amoeba*.

Jennings saw the scientific importance of keeping distinct "the results of observation and experiment from those of reasoning by analogy," but felt that we shouldn't ignore the possible subjective life of lower animals. To do so would suggest an indefensible gulf between the lower and higher forms, and it would not take into account the possible role of mental life in the explanation of behavior. We don't infer consciousness in a stone, said Jennings, because this wouldn't help us to control the stone's behavior; but the assumption of consciousness in a dog is *useful*, permitting us to "appreciate, foresee, and control its actions much more readily than we could otherwise do so."[5] If an amoeba were as large as a whale, we might infer from its actions "the same fundamental impulses as higher beasts of prey."

In a manner reminiscent of Romanes, Jennings says that in other organisms than ourselves we must judge the similarity of their psychic states to ours by the behavior that they show. Thus, we infer *perception* of an object from an animal's reaction to it; *discrimination*, when it responds in different ways to different objects; and *choice*, when the reaction is positive to some things, but negative or absent to others. *Attention*, he says, is based on the fact that one stimulus controls the behavior, even though other stimuli may be present.

"In fear," according to Jennings, "there is . . . a negative reaction to a representative stimulus—one that *stands* for a really injurious stimulation"; and *memory*, in general, is shown when behavior changes in accordance with "past stimuli received or past reactions given" so that the animal will react more adequately to the conditions that obtain. (*Associative memory*, a special case, is described in behavioral terms that either Loeb or Pavlov would have readily accepted.)

[5] H. S. Jennings, *Behavior of the Lower Organisms*, 1906, (p. 337)

In this attempt by Jennings to tell us what specific behavior goes with what specific state of mind, a new possibility is suggested. The door is opened, unwittingly, to those who would dispense with "psychic fictions" altogether. Could it not be argued that attention, perception, memory, and the like are simply words to be defined in certain behavioral terms, without any nece.   v reference to mental life at all? Jennings would not have agreed wi   such a proposition, since consciousness, for him, served a real purpose; and many others would have sided with him.

There was a growing tendency, however, to seek objective *evidence* of mental life in animals. Thorndike was interested in this problem (as mentioned on p. 42) when he began his famous studies, and so were a number of others. Especially worthy of mention here is Leonard Trelawney Hobhouse (1864–1929), who lived in the days of both Jennings and Thorndike, and whose contribution to our science has often been neglected.

Hobhouse was an Englishman and a sociologist, who was at one time or another a teacher of philosophy, an editorial writer (for the *Manchester Guardian*), and a political liberal, whose scholarly background in Darwinism, psychology, and philosophy led him to theorize extensively about man's social behavior and the structure of society. His most famous book, for us, is *Mind in Evolution*, first published in 1901. In this important book, Hobhouse discusses various kinds of adjustment in animals and man, from the instinct and the reflex to the highest level of intelligent adaptation.

In his treatment of *intelligence*, Hobhouse reminds us in many ways of Thorndike, with whose work he was acquainted, but which he felt was not complete. Intelligence, he says, works in two different ways—through *assimilation* and through *practical judgment*. In the first case, there is a stimulus, a reaction, and a *consequence*. The sight of a tiny object causes a baby chick to peck. If the object is food, a pleasant taste results, swallowing takes place, the pecking reaction is "confirmed," and is more likely to occur in the future. If the object is a caterpillar, however, a bad taste may result, and the pecking is "inhibited"—that is, there are movements of rejection, incompatible with those of swallowing and digestion, which will inhibit the latter if a similar stimulus object presents itself again.[6]

Assimilation thus involves the selective modification of behavior through confirmation or inhibition–Hobhouse's equivalents of reward and punishment. But there is a second way, neglected by Thorndike, in which intelligence works in animals–namely, through practical judgment. What Thorndike failed to test, says Hobhouse, was the ability of animals to deal with the *relations* that exist among the objects of their world.

He then goes on to argue that three levels may be distinguished in an organism's response to such relations: (1) he may react to them *without awareness*–the lowest level; (2) he may be *aware* of the relations, and thus possess what Hobhouse calls "concrete experience"; or (3) he may be aware of *relations in the abstract* and may be able to *compare them*–a stage that can be reached by man alone.

These levels were not without some basis in actual observation. They were derived in good part from the results of experiments that Hobhouse himself conducted with a number of animal species–cats, dogs, otters, even elephants, as well as a monkey and a chimpanzee. Like Thorndike, a couple of years before him, Hobhouse was looking for evidence of mental events in terms of observed behavior, and he developed a number of ingenious tests which he felt that animals could solve only through awareness of the relations of objects to each other.

Hobhouse's "experimental situations" were generally designed to test the ability of an animal to grasp the relation between some end and the means of its attainment. Thus, a lure of food might be accessible to one of his experimental subjects only when it pushed aside an obstacle, climbed upon a stool, "raked" it in with a stick, or pulled on a string to which it was attached. The special form of the

[6] In his *Evolution of Animal Intelligence* (1911), S. J. Holmes wrote, with respect to this example: "If a person is confronted with a sight of some nauseating medicine he has recently taken, avoiding or rejection movements are set up, such as making a face, or even retching movements of the stomach. Is it not these movements or attempts at movements that really inhibit the taking of medicine?"

tests that he used depended, of course, upon the specific sensory and motor equipment with which his subjects were endowed.

Hobhouse concluded, from his investigations, that animals as low in the evolutionary scale as the cat possessed a form of practical judgment—some awareness of relations. His best results, however, were obtained from his chimpanzee (the Professor) and his rhesus monkey, Jimmy. The Professor, for example, quickly learned to use a stick for raking pieces of banana to a point outside his cage where he could reach it with his hand. More than this, he would use a short stick for raking in a longer one with which he would then rake in the fruit. Jimmy was equally adept. When a piece of bread was placed beyond his grasp outside the cage and he was given a child's skipping rope, he would cast at the bread with one of the wooden handles of the rope until he brought it within reach.

When a piece of onion was placed on a table, also out of Jimmy's reach, he was able to solve his problem by dragging a box or chair into position so that he could climb upon it and thus attain his objective. Or, if he were unable to reach a piece of potato because his chain had to pass around a heavy box, he wasted little time before going back to the box and pulling it aside, thus lengthening the chain and securing the food. The solutions to these problems were often quite abrupt, unlike the gradual improvement that Thorndike had described. Also, once a problem had been mastered, it was solved almost immediately on later occasions when it was presented.[7]

Hobhouse sought evidence, as already noted, for an *awareness of relations* on the part of his animal subjects, something which he felt that Thorndike had neglected. Whether or not he found such evidence may be a matter for debate, but he did point up a fact that has since been widely recognized—the stimulus situation to which an organism may react is sometimes very difficult to describe. If

[7] Hobhouse's problem situations, with but one or two exceptions, were later used by Professor Köhler, the *Gestalt* psychologist (see chapter 10), for a similar purpose, in his tests for the presence of "insight" in chimpanzees. A fascinating account of his studies is found in Köhler's well-known book, *The Mentality of Apes* (1925).

Hobhouse did not solve the problem of response-to-relations, he at least made it clear that a problem existed.

The attempt to find behavioral grounds for mental events did not come to an end with Hobhouse. Students of comparative psychology concerned themselves with this matter well into the present century. Elaborate attempts were made by leaders in the field to establish satisfactory criteria of mind (consciousness, awareness, etc.) in various organisms, based not only on behavior, but on structure (an animal without an eye could not have *visual* experience). Lloyd Morgan's canon was examined and reexamined, as were the pronouncements of Loeb, Jennings, and others. What had seemed so simple to Charles Darwin, turned out to be enormously complex.[8]

There was no serious thought, however, of renouncing the study of mind—especially the human mind—in favor of a more objective, less debatable, natural science of behavior. The teachings of Descartes and the "mental philosophers," the tenets of early psychophysiology, and the systematic views of Wilhelm Wundt had left an imprint that was not to be easily erased. Before the full effect of reflex physiology, evolution, and animal behavior study could be felt within our province, we had to go through a turbulent period of opposing viewpoints—a period of disputation, logical assessment, and vain attempts at reconciliation. This was the era of psychological schools, which may be said to have begun in the early years of this century and lasted well into the 1930s, or beyond.

---

[8] Consider, for example, the following substitute for Lloyd Morgan's canon, proposed as recently as 1928: "Any experience or mental process in another organism can be inferred from structure, situation, history, and behavior only when a similar experience or mental process is or has been invariably associated with similar structure, situation, history, and behavior in oneself; and the degree of probability of the inference will be proportional to the degree of similarity." (D. K. Adams, *Psychological Review*, Vol. 35, 1928.) Such requirements should discourage one from guessing about the mental life of animals, or even other human beings!

7

TITCHENER
AND STRUCTURALISM

Edward Bradford Titchener (1867–1927) was an Englishman by birth, a German by temperament, and an American by residence. He came to Leipzig in 1890, after a brilliant student career at Oxford, to learn at first hand about the new psychology. He had already translated into English the third edition of the *Physiological Psychology*. In two years' time he took his doctorate and accepted a call to America to take charge of Cornell University's new laboratory of experimental psychology. There he remained for the rest of his life, 35 years, without becoming naturalized—in either a civic or academic sense.

At Cornell, Titchener did full credit to his master. He carried on the Wundtian tradition in the Wundtian manner—teaching, writing, and directing research—and with extraordinary ability. His scholarship was profound; his lectures and his writings were models of clear and dignified exposition; his personality was magnetic and forceful. Undergraduates flocked to his classes and graduates came to his laboratory. Cornell was soon the headquarters and clearinghouse for a very important branch of experimental psychology in America. Titchener's may not have been the only psychology on this side of the Atlantic, but for two or three decades it was the best organized, most articulate, and the closest to the pattern set by Wundt. In our search for a definition of psychology we may profitably examine this Leipzig-Cornell product in some detail, to see what Titchener thought psychology was.

Titchener's view changed somewhat from year to year, but we can get a very good notion of his principal systematic ideas from two of his published texts: *A Textbook of Psychology* (1910) and *A Beginner's Psychology* (1915). In these books, written primarily for sophomores and freshmen respectively, we shall find a more outspoken account than in some of his more advanced delineations for his colleagues. "Psychology is the science of the mind." This is the general statement with which Titchener begins his systematic account. But he hastens to add that this statement is easily misinterpreted by "common sense," and he goes on to qualify it in certain ways. "The mind with which psychology deals must be a mind that is describable in terms of observed fact"; it must not be identified with some insubstantial little being inside of our heads. In order to come nearer to a truly scientific understanding of the term, Titchener then makes a distinction between the world of physics and the world of psychology. Let us read again from the *Beginner's* text.

The world of physics is colourless, toneless, neither cold nor warm; its spaces are always of the same extent, its times are always of the same duration, its mass is invariable; it would be just what it is now if mankind were swept from the face of the earth. For what is light in the textbooks of physics?—a train of electro-magnetic waves; and sound is a vibratory motion of air and water; and heat is a dance of molecules; and all these things are independent of man.

Physics views the world with man "left out," so to speak; psychology, on the other hand, describes the world as it is in man's experience—it views the world with man "left in."

The world of psychology contains looks and tones and feels; it is the world of dark and light, of noise and silence, of rough and smooth; its space is sometimes large and sometimes small, as everyone knows who in adult life has gone back to his childhood's home; its time is sometimes short and sometimes long; it has no invariables. It contains also the thoughts, emotions, memories, imaginations, volitions that you naturally ascribe to mind . . . mind is simply the *inclusive name of all these phenomena*.

From these quotations it should not be concluded that there is any fundamental difference between the *experience* of the physicist and that of the psychologist. Titchener was not denying that the physicist had experience; he was merely emphasizing the well-known fact that the physicist's *description* of his world was in terms of conceptual things like electromagnetic waves, vibratory motions, and molecules. He might logically have gone further and made it clearer that the psychologist also describes *his* world in conceptual terms; but this is a subtle matter and we need not stop to quibble here.

Titchener tells us next that in the *physical* world there are such objects as human bodies, with nervous systems that organize them into single, integrated, organic wholes. We have learned from a variety of sources that the "phenomena" of psychology are to be related to certain activities of these nervous systems. For example, destruction of some portion of the brain is frequently tied up with the loss of some form of experience, say visual. Likewise, disturbance in experience, or lack of experience, may denote the loss of certain brain function. The "man left in" is, then, little more than the nervous system itself. Psychology might even be defined as the study of mind (experience, phenomena) *considered as dependent upon the nervous system*; for wherever we find experience or mental phenomena we also find a nervous system. Not all nervous events are paralleled by mental ones, but everything mental has its counterpart in something physical happening in the brain as a result of stimulation of sense organs and nerves.

The reader need not despair if this reasoning seems somewhat complicated. Much of it will be cleared up as we go into the less abstract details of Titchener's psychology. It may merely be noted in passing that there is implied in all this a philosophical dualism, a distinction between body and mind, that harks back to Wundt and beyond—even to Descartes, although Titchener would not have subscribed to interactionism.

The *method* of psychology is our next consideration. Mind, to be studied scientifically, must be observed. Observation is the *sine qua non* of all science. Titchener felt, with Wundt, that *having* experience was very close to observing it; and he stressed the method of introspection. But his formula for introspective observation was more comprehensive than Wundt's, and it gives us a basis for distinguishing psychological from physical observation. He points out that *all* scientific observation requires three things: a certain *attitude* towards one's experience, the *experiencing* itself, and an adequate *report* of the experience in words. Where the attitude is that of the psychologist we call the totality of the observational process "introspection"; where it is the attitude of the physicist that is involved we call the process "inspection"—or just plain "observation." Difference in attitude alone sets off the observations of the psychologist from those of any other scientist.

"Introspection" is an unfortunate word in that, because of its history and its everyday usage, it is open to misconstruction. Titchener realized this and took pains to show that it was *not* to be thought of as a reflection upon, or contemplation of, one's experience (as Descartes and the British empiricists would have considered it) or as a morbid sort of self-interest (for which a better term is "introversion"). In fact, Titchener was ever on the alert to show that scientific terms in general should always be used carefully and unequivocally, and he frequently pointed to the confusion that arose when "common-sense" meanings were given to scientific words.

When we read Titchener's statement of the *problem* of psychology, we see clearly the imprint of his Leipzig teachings. The problem is again threefold. There is, first, the *analysis of mental phenomena into their elements*. A description of any cross section of experience is bound to be an analysis, for we analyze whenever we describe—we break down the object of our observation into certain fundamental parts. (If the reader wishes to test the truth of this, let him try to describe any common object near at hand. Analyzing is one of the most natural human activities in the world, except that it is seldom carried so far as to become very scientific.)

Synthesis, although more difficult than analysis, goes hand in hand with it. It involves the study of the connections between the elementary mental processes and is the road to the determination of *laws of connection* of these processes. This is the second phase of our problem, and it answers the question "How?" just as analysis answers the question "What?"

The third aspect of the problem goes beyond the description of mind (and beyond Wundt's statement of the problem of psychology) to the *explanation* of mind. It aims to answer the question "Why?" and, in so doing, it appeals to the parallel events in the nervous system and its attached organs; it endeavors to *correlate mind with the nervous system*. Titchener denied that nervous activity was the *cause* of experience; but he affirmed that a thoroughgoing statement of the *conditions* or circumstances under which mental processes occurred demanded a reference to this activity, for explanation's sake. "Dew is formed under the condition of a difference of temperature between the air and the ground; ideas are formed under the condition of certain processes in the nervous system."

So much for the statement of the fundamental premises of the Titchenerian system. We are now entitled to examine the results of such an attack upon the fortress of mind, to see how the system handled the experimental research that was the real basis of the new psychology.

Introspective analysis, said Titchener, brings to light three main classes of mental elements. (This number decreased with the development of Titchener's ideas; we take them as of 1910.) These classes are *sensations, images, and affections (feelings)*. They may be dealt with in this order.

"Sensations are . . . the characteristic elements of perceptions, of the sights, sounds and similar experiences due to our present surroundings." They may be divided into various *modalities* or departments according to (1) their introspective similarities (e.g., a tone is more like a noise than it is like a taste); (2) the sense organs upon whose functions they are conditioned (e.g., there is eye sensation and ear sensation); or (3) the types of stimuli which condition them, located either within or without the organism. Titchener depends mainly upon their introspective differences in classifying the departments but uses the other methods when satisfactory group names are lacking.

The principal modalities of sensory elements are then listed. We find seven in all: the visual, auditory, olfactory, gustatory, cutaneous, kinesthetic, and organic senses. Each of these, in turn, may undergo further analysis and subdivision. Thus, vision yields color and light—chromatic and achromatic—sensations; audition yields tones and noises; and smell gives us a variety of sensations that may be placed in somewhat distinct groups (such as fragrant, spicy, and foul odors) on the basis of similarity and difference. Cutaneous sensations are divisible into sensations of pressure (true touch), cold, warmth, and pain; and kinesthesis, the old *muscle* sense, shows itself to contain muscle, tendon, and joint components. Organic turns out to be a general term for all those ill-defined sensations arising from the digestive, urinary, circulatory, respiratory, and genital systems.

A word of qualification may be appropriate at this point. Titchener did not *discover* these sensations. Neither did he discover the laws of their relation to environmental stimuli, with which he deals extensively in his texts. This work of discovery, classification, and correlation had been started ages before, even in Aristotle's day, and had reached a high degree of exactitude in the studies of the 19th-century physiologists whose work has already been mentioned. What Titchener did was just what other systematists had done, and still do: he appropriated these facts (adding items from his own laboratory) and arranged them within his system—for their better integration and illumination.

From Titchener's point of view, sensations were mental elements comparable to the elements of chemistry. One defines chemical elements by reference to certain properties, such as their power of reflecting light, their specific gravity, their fusibility, etc. In the same manner one may characterize mental elements by reference to certain properties that they possess or do not possess. Thus we arrive at Titchener's notion of *attributes*.

Sensations, as irreducible units of the mental world, possess certain characteristics to which we refer when we want to describe these units in minute detail. For example, all sensations, of whatever sort and from whatever source, possess the attribute of *quality*. This is the attribute by virtue of which we *name* sensations. B-flat, pink, warm, and sour are such qualities, and they serve to distinguish one sensation from another.

A second attribute of all sensations is *intensity*. This is recognized whenever we consider the strength or degree of a sensation. A tone may be loud or faint, a pressure light or heavy, an odor weak or strong; we are aided in our description by these intensive character-istics. Incidentally, it was this attribute of intensity with which Fechner dealt most in his psychophysical studies, for it lends itself readily to quantitative statement. Theoretically, although not practically, any sensation might even be given a numerical designa-tion on a graded scale from least to most intense.

Quality and intensity are the most important attributes of sensation, but there are others. Titchener lists these, in 1915, as duration, vividness, and extension.[1] *Duration* refers to the time aspect of sensations: "it is the bare going on, going forward, keeping like itself, that may be observed in any and every sensation." *Vividness* is difficult to describe: "if you want to know how . . . vividness feels . . . observe your mental processes now, as you are puzzling over this book; the difference between foreground and background, focus and margin—between the dominant ideas aroused by what you read, and the obscure perceptions derived from your surroundings—will show itself at any rate in the rough." *Extension* is the elementary space factor in experience, just as duration is the elementary time factor; "it is the basis . . . of our perceptions of form, size, distance, locality, direction"; the tiniest star in the evening sky, or the raindrop on the outstretched hand—both have perceptible size.

The first four of these attributes-quality, intensity, duration, and vividness—are properties of all sensations; but only visual and cutaneous elements, such as colors and pressures, clearly possess an extensive attribute, the removal of which would nullify the sensation itself.

Furthermore, even such a simple attribute as quality may itself be a resultant of two or three distinct attributes, the detection of which is the very ultimate in introspective analysis. The visual quality "red," for example, is a combination of such attributes as saturation, brilliance, and hue, all of which are qualitative. We need not, however, go into these more delicate matters here. There are other mental elements than sensations to be considered in this survey of Titchener's teachings.

[1] Later they became respectively "protensity," "attensity," and "extensity."

David Hume, as we have seen, was one of the first to distinguish between sensations and images, calling them respectively "impressions" and "ideas," and thinking of the latter as "faint copies" of the former. But Hume was also shrewd and observing enough to see that it was often difficult to tell the two apart on the basis of experience alone:

It is not impossible but in particular instances they may very nearly approach to each other. Thus in sleep, in a fever, in madness, or in any very violent emotions of the soul, our ideas may approach to our impressions: As on the other hand it sometimes happens, that our impressions are so faint and low, that we cannot distinguish them from our ideas.

Except for the minor difference of terminology this states almost exactly the position of Titchener, 176 years later, with respect to the question of sensations and images as mental elements of equal dignity and rating. He goes a few steps beyond Hume, however, when he says, in the *Beginner's Psychology*, that "it is very doubtful if there is any real psychological difference between sensation and image"; but, like Hume, he falls back upon a nonpsychological difference in defining the image as "an elementary mental process, akin to sensation and perhaps indistinguishable from it, which persists when the sensory stimulus is withdrawn or appears when the sensory stimulus is absent."

If this seems obscure to the reader, let him recall that the psychologist's function, according to Titchener, was to describe experience, and experience alone. Stimuli are *not* mental processes, although they may give rise to them and may be considered in relation to them. Thus, when he says that sensations and images are perhaps indistinguishable, he means only that on the basis of introspective observation *alone* we cannot tell the difference: nothing about the mental process itself says "I am sensation" or "I am image." (Whether Titchener took seriously his own suggestion, in another context, of an introspectively observable "textural" difference between the two, may remain an unanswered question.)

Titchener finds images for every sense, with the possible exception of kinesthesis, and he finds them of different kinds within a sense. Besides the visual, auditory, and other modality images, there are such types as *recurrent* images (e.g., the tune that runs in our heads), *hallucinatory* images (the doorbell's ring, when no one pushed it), *dream* images, *memory* images, and so on—the list is long. These images, like the sensations, have their attributes of quality, intensity, duration, and the like; and, with sensations, they go far towards supplying the elementary components of mental life.

There remains to be discussed Titchener's third class of elements—the *affections* or *simple feelings*. These are defined by contrast with the elementary process of sensation. An affection differs from a sensation in the number of attributes it possesses; it lacks clearness (vividness) and it lacks extension. It may vary in the length of time it occupies (duration); it may be of greater or less degree (intensity); and it always has one of two qualities—*pleasantness* and *unpleasantness*. Never do these two qualities exist at the same time (there are no "mixed" feelings); and never must this form of feeling be confused with the "feelings" of the popular vocabulary. When we say "this feels rough or smooth," "I feel good," or "he feels that I am right," we are trying to make the term fit experiences that are far more complicated in their nature and in which true feeling (affection) plays at best an inconsiderable role. (Obviously, we should not confuse this "affection" with that of the lover-sweetheart or parent-child relationship, no matter how much pleasantness and unpleasantness either may involve.)

In his treatment of affection Titchener departs vigorously from Wundt's teachings. The latter had been unwilling to recognize the status of pleasantness and unpleasantness as qualities of elementary processes, and had given equal rank to such feelings as tension and relaxation, excitement and calm. Titchener examines Wundt's theory in detail, as well as the experimental evidence behind it, and comes out for the elementary character of affections alone, and the combination-character of Wundt's other categories of feeling. He argues that tension, relaxation, excitement, and calm are really "sense feelings," combinations of organic sensations and true feelings.[2]

[2] The controversy between pupil and master need not detain us here. Besides, Titchener, before his death, had reached the conclusion that even the feelings of pleasantness and unpleasantness were probably reducible to sensations.

So much for mental analysis. As we turn from the elements of Titchener's system to the combinations of these elements we go from the simple to the complex. We deal with such mental structures as perceptions, ideas, and emotions; with association, memory, and thought; even with such complicated things as sentiments and the *self*. Full justice cannot be rendered to all these topics here, but certain general principles may be outlined and illustrative material presented that should help the reader to get the feel of the Titchenerian system.

Perceptions and *ideas* come up for consideration first. They are matters of everyday experience that offer themselves for analysis. Only when we take the laboratory attitude do we appreciate their compound nature. They are the units of our daily mental life just as sensations, images, and feelings are the units of psychological analysis. The perceptions may be analyzed, with careful introspection, into (1) a number of sensations which are supplemented by (2) various images and (3) "moulded by the action of nerve forces which show themselves neither in sensation nor in image." It is to be noticed that only the first two of these characteristics are really "experiential"; the third is an inference, not a true mental content but something lying *behind* it. An example: the *core* of our experience of, say, a tree is no more than an arrangement of color sensations. With this sensation-core come certain supplementary images—it is the tree that shades our neighbor's flower-bed in summer, the tree that caused the lawsuit, the tree that wore "a nest of robins in her hair." Moreover, the tree is taken automatically to be a real "thing" occupying real "space"; and this characterization may be founded upon no mental content whatever—either sensation or image—but be due merely to a kind of brain-habit that lacks a representative in the assembly of elements.

Just as a perception is a compound affair in which sensation figures prominently, so a typical idea is a mental structure possessing a nucleus of *images*. "Last winter's snow may come to us . . . as a visual picture, an uneven spread of white, with streaks of grey-brown on the peaks and along the valleys, honeycombed and broken from some partial thaw." This is the imaginal core—the basic image-content of the idea. But there is more. Other images may cluster about this core: "we recall the day so-and-so got his feet wet, or the big fall of that December Thursday." Even this is not all. "We can hardly think of getting our feet wet . . . without some actual movement that arouses sensation." The idea may, then, include sensation material that adds to its complexity. Finally, as in perception a "brain-habit" may lie behind our idea as a molding or determining factor.

Feelings (pleasantness and unpleasantness), combined at an elementary level with certain sensations, primarily kinesthetic and organic, give us "sense feelings." There are six classes of these sense feelings: the exciting and the calming, the straining and the relaxing, and the agreeable and the disagreeable, each dependent upon the peculiar nature of the sensation-feeling blend. Each may combine, in turn, with further sensory and imaginal processes under certain conditions to produce such *emotions* as joy and fear, anger and grief, hope and relief.

There is no need of going further with this aspect of psychological compounding. Its general nature and the direction it took should by now be clear; and there are two or three other matters that are worthy of a brief review before we conclude our inspection of the house that Titchener built.

The first of these concerns a question that was asked, and answered, as long ago as 1709, in Bishop Berkeley's *New Theory of Vision*, and a quotation from the good Bishop's writings will introduce us to the problem here.

Sitting in my study I hear a coach drive along the street; I look through the casement and see it; I walk out and enter it. Thus, common speech would incline one to think I heard, saw, and touched the same thing, to wit, the coach. It is nevertheless certain the ideas intromitted by each sense are widely different and distinct from each other; but, having been observed constantly to go together, they are spoken of as one and the same thing.

Berkeley offers this merely as an example of the manner in which "mind" generates "matter" (more specifically, "things" or "objects") by the combination or association of certain ideas. We have already had an illustration of the same kind of reasoning in his theory of distance perception. The student of history, however, may find in this quotation an anticipation of a much better known theory—namely, Titchener's "*context theory of meaning*."[3]

An obvious characteristic of our perceptions and ideas, according to Titchener, is that they have meaning. Last winter's snow, the tree in the yard, the rumble of Bishop Berkeley's coach—these are meaningful events. But what, psychologically, i.e., introspectively, is meaning? The answer to this question may already have been given in my discussion of perception and idea, but it will do no harm to elaborate.

When we analyze mind introspectively we find, not meanings, but mental processes—sensations, images, feelings, and their combinations. The tree of our example we found to be so much sensation, *plus* an accretion of images; last winter's snow turned out to be so much image, *plus* more imagery and sensation. It is in this plus-factor of mental processes that we shall find the answer to our question.

"Meaning," says Titchener, ". . . is always context; one mental process is the meaning of another mental process if it is that other's context." Context itself is nothing more than "the fringe of related processes that gathers about the central group of sensations or images." In perception and in idea there is *core plus context*, and the latter "carries" the meaning of the former, i.e., it is what we find when we scrutinize experience in our search for the counterpart of everyday logical meaning.

Titchener offers a number of illustrations to show the wisdom of this core-context distinction. Context may, in some cases, be stripped from the core—as when we repeat aloud some word until the context disappears and the word becomes meaningless; context may be added to core—as when we learn the meaning of some strange design or foreign word; context and core may be disjoined in

---

[3] It may help, in this discussion, to parallel Berkeley's example with another. I hear the sound of a bark, and I say "there's my dog"; in the distance I see a moving object of a familiar shape, I say "my dog"; I feel a cold wetness on my exposed ear as I lie in bed in the morning, "my dog"; I smell a pungent barnyard odor, and again I say "my dog." The sensory core of these perceptions is different in each case, coming as it does from a different sense-department; but each perception *means* "my dog." *Why* it does so is the question that now concerns us.

time—as when we know what we want to say but need time to find expressive words, or when the point of a joke is delayed in appearance; the same core may have several contexts—as implied in our worry about the true meaning of a chance remark; the same context may accrue to different cores—as in the case of Bishop Berkeley's coach; and so on. Titchener did not lack for examples to support his distinction. His inability, however, to demonstrate that meaning was *always* context is seen in his admission that it might be carried by a "brain-set" in the absence of conscious representation—as when the skilled reader grasps the meaning of a printed page, or a musical composition is rendered in the appropriate key, *without* the presence of a fringe of images to supplement the core of the perception.

Context accrues to core *associatively*. Titchener made no outright statement to this effect, but it is clear that we can understand such compounding in no other fashion. We may, then, briefly inspect Thitchener's treatment of association as a psychological principle, and thereby see what happened to the old British doctrine in the hands of an experimentalist.

"Whenever a sensory or imaginal process occurs in consciousness, there are likely to appear with it (of course, in imaginal terms) all those sensory and imaginal processes which occurred together with it in any earlier conscious present." This statement, which is Titchener's fundamental law of association, is taken from the *Textbook* of 1910, where it is preceded by a painstaking criticism of the older associationists and followed by an elaborate set of qualifying and amplifying clauses which we need not consider here. It is meant to be a *descriptive* formula for the observed facts of the older doctrine; Titchener's *explanatory* formula appeals to the neural events running parallel to the sensory and imaginal processes mentioned above.

The Law of Association became very important in Titchener's system, particularly in his treatment of memory and imagination, but Titchener himself realized that it was not all-sufficient for the understanding of mental connections. This realization is apparent in the very wording of the law. Note that he says "are *likely* to appear" (my italics) when he speaks of the associated sensory and imaginal processes. Remember, too, his use of a "brain-habit" as a molding or determining factor in the construction of perceptions and ideas. This amounts to a recognition that mental processes, and actions as well, arise not only as a result of the strength of associative bonds, but also because of certain directive forces—"brain-habits," "instinctive tendencies," "nervous sets," and so on—that may even work against the influence of oft-repeated associations. Thus, in addition to associative tendencies, we have *determining* tendencies (and we are reminded of Hobbes, with his "Traynes of Thought" that were guided by *desire* or *purpose*.) Sensory and imaginal processes which, on the basis of frequent past association, should be joined together in the mind may, because of the pressure of a determining tendency, be kept apart. A simple example: the word *black* might, by virtue of association, call up *white* in the reader's mind, and *bitter* might call up *sweet*; but what would have happened if he had been told ("set" or "determined") in advance to find *rhymes* for *black* and *bitter*?

Our present purpose does not demand a more comprehensive and complete portrayal of Titchener's point of view. I have set down here, in spite of what the specialist might tritely call "glaring omissions," a working outline of his system—enough, at least, to provide us with a scheme of reference when we examine other views. There is experience (mental process); it is to be analyzed introspectively into elements (sensations, images, and feelings), with their attributes (quality, intensity, and so forth). The elements are fused or patterned in space and time (associated) to give us such mental structures as perceptions, ideas, sense feelings, emotions, and the like. Finally, these processes—both the simple and the complex—are paralleled by events in the nervous system and, to some extent, determined by them.

This Leipzig-Cornell product—by Titchener out of Wundt—was for more than two decades the psychology against which other psychologies matched themselves. As a system or school it came to be known principally as "structural" or "introspective" psychology—for reasons that should be clear with a moment's reflection, and will be even clearer later on. The most recent label, advanced by Titchener himself, is "existential," a word chosen to emphasize the fact that the world of mental process ("bare existence") is the only world that science can know.

8

AMERICA
AND FUNCTIONALISM

The shifting ground, the new discoveries, the changing values—even the fads and fancies—of any young science make it very unlikely that a given school of thought will last for long, to the exclusion of all others. Certainly it will not survive without invasion in some quarters and rebellion in others; and especially will this be true in a country where there is notably a fine disdain for precedent and a high regard for the practical. It was not to be expected that the Titchenerian dogma should go unchallenged in America.

The attack upon the orderly, disciplined ranks of structural psychology was typically early-American. It came from no single, united front, under command of a single recognized leader. Instead there was guerilla warfare, with many chieftains, striking in from many points of vantage, with many weapons.

This rebel psychology may or may not have been a school, or even a system, in the strict sense of these words, but it was undeniably an important *movement* and we cannot ignore it in our search for psychology's definition. Its doctrines are presented in no single text by no one outstanding sponsor, but they played a great part in determining the form and content of present-day psychology. If, then, in what follows, this movement is referred to as a "school" or "system," no grave injustice will be done.

Functional psychology took its form in the hands of a number of Americans, in particular a small group of antistructuralists at the University of Chicago, during the closing years of the last century and the opening years of this. John Dewey (1859–1952), James R. Angell (1869–1949), and Harvey Carr (1873–1954) are the principal names, but there were numerous others whose interests and sympathies (or antagonisms) inclined them in the same direction. These men were seldom in complete agreement as to systematic doctrine, and they do not seem to have worried much about the matter, yet there were certain general characteristics that marked them as a group.

(1) They were opposed to structuralism, of either the Wundtian or Titchenerian sort. Theirs was the first active protest in this country against the kind of psychology that blossomed in the Leipzig laboratory and seemed in the way of becoming the *only* psychology in Germany and America. The reason for this protest will soon be apparent.

(2) They were interested in what the mind *is for*, rather than what it *is*–the *function* of mind rather than its *structure*. They sought to answer such questions as these: What do mental processes accomplish? What difference do mental processes make? How do mental processeses work?

(3) They were a practical-minded group, not above joining hands on a common sense basis of values. Titchener had little respect for common sense and tried valiantly to keep the skirts of the new psychology clear of the purely useful. The functionalists had no such compunctions; both Dewey and Angell ultimately deserted psychology for practical, i.e., educational pursuits, and others of the group showed similar leanings.

(4) They represented the biological rather than the physiological tradition in psychology. They were influenced less by the careful laboratory studies of 19th century physiology than they were by the stimulating concepts of Darwinian biology. Impressed by the ideas of mental evolution and "survival of the fittest," they sought to determine the place occupied by mind in helping the human or animal organism to hold its own in the struggle for existence.

(5) They demanded that the field of psychology be broadened to include the methods and findings of animal, child, abnormal,

differential, and other types of psychological research—research that was attracting more and more the attention of serious-minded students in this country and abroad, but which had never quite achieved respectability in the classrooms of structuralism.

(6) Finally, these men were, at one time or another, directly or indirectly under the influence of a man who has properly been called the "dean" of American psychologists, a man who is a symbol of the very best in functionalism without being a real member of this or any other school.

William James (1842–1910) cannot be pigeonholed for purposes such as ours. Physiologist, psychologist, philosopher, teacher, writer—these are pitifully inexpressive titles for this genius of the Western Hemisphere. The reader will have to go to James himself[1]—for instance, to his *Principles of Psychology*—if he wants to feel the force of his personality and appreciate the effect of his teachings upon the character and destiny of American psychology.

It will have to suffice, in this context, to note that James opposed the "brass-instrument"[2] psychology of Wundt, with its hair-splitting dissection of mental content; argued that mind was a "personal," "changing," "continuous," and "selective" agent, "dealing with objects other than itself"; and promoted the Darwinian view that it had evolved for the purpose of "steering a nervous system grown too complex to regulate itself." And he did all this, and more, with so much skill and vigor, with such neatly chosen testimony and so many lively illustrations, that no intellectually alert American—after 1890, when *The Principles* was published—could very well ignore him. He did not establish a school, or belong to one; his system was his own, and he never "promoted" it. His interests led him soon to other fields. He left, however, an indelible, though indescribable, mark upon the new psychology.

With these general characteristics of functionalism in mind, we may now consider the system itself. This will not be an easy task, and fault may be found with this account because it has been

[1] Or to Professor R. B. Perry's excellent two-volume book, *The Thought and Character of William James* (Little, Brown, and Company, Boston, 1936).

[2] "Brass-instrument" is a facetious characterization of that kind of psychology which utilizes the apparatus and techniques of the physiologist or physicist in the investigation of mind.

necessary to pick and choose from various sources to show the distinctive qualities of the system. Among the members of the functionalist group there was no great stress upon system as system, and no such unanimity of belief—I might almost say, horror of heresy—as prevailed in the camp of structuralism.

The *subject-matter* of psychology, to the functionalist, was *mental activity*. This is a term employed by Carr, one of the most systematic of the group, who did much to crystallize and modify the school's teachings for wide-spread consumption. Mental activity is a broad term, not to be confused with Titchener's *mental process*. It refers to such processes as thinking, feeling, imagining, perceiving, and the like; *not* to such elementary processes as *red*, *sweet*, or *B-flat*, or even the perceptual and imaginal complexes of which they are components.

Mental activities are definitely distinct, but very elastic, categories. Each individual mental activity may involve any number of mental contents such as the structuralist described, none of which need be exactly duplicated from observation to observation. Thus, a given activity such as "thinking" might never be reinstated with the same content of ideas or images; but "thinking" as a *function* of the human organism might be repeated again and again. We might, for example, "think through" a certain mathematical problem many times without ever using the same mental images, yet the function involved would be the same with respect to the most important factor—the arrival at a correct solution.

Moreover, mental activity is described as *psychophysical* activity. This conception, sometimes difficult for even the advanced student to comprehend, is central to functionalistic doctrine. Dewey argued that the mental and physical aspects of experience could not be treated as distinct in psychology. In the words of one reviewer: "mental acts are not psychical events pure and simple; they are events in which both the physical and the psychical are present."[3] Carr writes to the same purpose when he says that mental activities "are not only experienced, but they are also reactions of a physical organism . . . . They are acts of which the individual has some knowledge . . . that directly involve such structures as the sense organs, muscles, and nerves." Neither of these eminent functionalists

---

[3] Edna Heidbreder, *Seven Psychologies* (The Century Co., 1933), p. 213.

would admit the fruitfulness, for psychology, of any sharp split between the body and the mind.

The *methods* of psychology, according to such a functionalist as Angell, are *introspection*, or "subjective observation," and the *objective observation* of physical science. Carr says: "Objective observation refers to the apprehension of the mental operations of another individual in so far as these are reflected in his behavior. Subjective observation refers to the apprehension of one's own mental operations."

The advantages and disadvantages of each type of observation are discussed by Carr in his *Psychology* (1925). He points out that, whereas introspection provides a "more intimate and comprehensive knowledge of mental events," it is a difficult form of observation for the average person. The kaleidoscopic changes in the mental life elude all but the trained observer, and even *his* report is unverifiable because of its essentially personal nature. The objective method should, wherever possible, supplement the subjective, and it is obviously preferable in studying animals, children, primitive peoples, and the insane.

The *problem* of psychology, for the functionalist, seems, at the first blush, to resemble that of structuralism; both seek answers to the queries "What?", "How?", and "Why?" But scrutiny reveals a significant difference in the meaning of these questions for the rival camps. We are already familiar with the threefold Titchenerian statement of the problem—"analysis into elements," "laws of connection," and "correlation of mind and nervous system." Functionalism presents the matter in an entirely different way.

Generally speaking, it may be said that the functionalist's task is to discover (1) *how* mental activity goes on, (2) *what* it accomplishes, and (3) *why* it takes place. All three phases of the problem are but aspects of a single, comprehensive relationship between organism and environment—a relationship that will become clearer when we consider two concepts that resulted from the functionalist's way of thinking about psychological matters: the "reflex arc" concept, and the concept of "adaptive behavior."

The reader already knows the reflex story, as told in chapter 4, from Descartes to Sherrington and Pavlov. He has seen how the concept was refined and expanded to include more and more of the behavior of animals, even intact animals, within a laboratory setting.

By 1925, the view had taken hold in many quarters that behavior could be analyzed into reflex elements or units. Some objectively oriented psychologists were beginning to use the reflex as an explanatory principle. It seemed that human behavior itself might be treated in terms of reflex chains and patterns, or elementary reflex arcs.

Functional psychologists were interested in conduct as well as consciousness—in physical as well as psychical activity. Moreover, they believed that many truly psychological events had no appreciable mental aspect. It came very natural to them to accept the reflex-arc concept, and they did so, but only with such reservations as were necessary to make it compatible with, and illustrate, their general point of view.

According to Carr, three principles may be deduced from the reflex-arc concept. The first is that "all sensory stimuli exert some effect upon the activity of the organism"; the second is that "all activity . . . is initiated by sensory stimuli"; and the third is that "there is a continuous process of interaction between sensory stimuli and motor response."

In connection with the first of these principles Carr reminds the reader that, in the environment of any individual, there are countless physical changes of greater or less degree. When some of these changes are adequate to bring about changes in the individual's sense organs (organs of taste, smell, hearing, and so on), they may properly be called "sensory stimuli." These stimuli, acting upon the sense organs, always initiate activity that is passed along over the nerve paths to some muscle or gland, eliciting some sort of response in these structures. In certain cases the response is very noticeable, as when a person jumps from his bed at the sound of a bell or a motorist stops at the shift of a traffic light. In other cases the response may be so slight as to be detectible only by the most delicate of recording devices, as when the effect of a whispered threat or the tiniest prick of a pin can only be perceived as a change in the electrical resistance of a person's skin or in the quickening of his pulse. In *all* cases, however, according to this "principle of organic behavior," sensory stimuli evoke *some* sort of response.

The second principle is the corollary of the first, but is, perhaps, less acceptable to the reader's common sense point of view. It holds in effect, that there is *no* response without a stimulus, that muscular or glandular reactions may not be aroused by nerve impulses in the absence of some stimulus that releases the energy stored within the organism's "sensory-neuro-muscular" mechanism. This is an assumption that is not easily demonstrated. The initiating stimuli for many responses are very difficult, if not impossible, to discover. Carr points out that responses may be due to stimulation from *within* the organism—stimulation that acts upon the sense organs lying in the muscles and other internal bodily tissues. "For example, hunger, thirst, and internal pains are very powerful stimuli that largely determine the nature of the organism's reactions."

The third principle emphasizes the interplay between stimulus and response. "Every movement resulting from a sensory situation inevitably modifies that situation, and this change or modification of the sensory situation constitutes a new sensory stimulus which in turn modifies the act that produced it." This is an important component of the reflex-arc concept, for it stresses the fact that the nature of sensory stimuli depends upon the responses just as much as the nature of the responses depends upon the stimuli—a fact that must be considered in dealing with any sample of stimulus-response activity. An example: in the midst of writing this page I hear the ring of the doorbell (a change in my sensory situation); I get up from my chair and open the door of my room (responses to the change); from the living room below I hear the murmur of voices (my responses have provided new sensory stimuli); listening, I recognize the voice of a long-absent friend (my "listening" response changes the situation once more); and I hurry down the stairs (response to the new change). In this example there are many neglected stages, but it illustrates Carr's point—that every response alters the sensory situation and thus determines in part the nature of subsequent responses.

For purposes of analysis, we may be justified in dissecting the conduct of an organism into such units as those of the above example, but it is a matter of everyday observation that much of an organism's behavior possesses a character that our illustration did not bring into prominence—namely, the character of being *adaptive*; and this brings us to our second functionalistic concept.

"Adaptive behavior," according to Carr, involves "a motivating stimulus, a sensory situation, and a response that alters that situation in a way that satisfies the motivating conditions." This is the concept in a nutshell; and, to the reader who has fully grasped Carr's notion of the reflex arc, it should be apparent that the two concepts bear a strong resemblance to each other.

The new factor to be considered is the "motivating" stimulus, or condition, with which the second concept deals. A *motive*, to Carr, is always a stimulus—generally an internal one—and is practically identical with what some psychologists call "organic need," "urge," or "drive." He defines it as "a relatively persistent stimulus that dominates the behavior of an individual until he reacts in such a manner that he is no longer affected by it." What we call hunger, thirst, and the like would be typical examples—even the pain of a splinter in one's finger or the temperature of an overheated room. In fact, almost any stimulus might be a motive by virtue of its insistence or dominance, or because of the organism's readiness to react to it. The steady drip of water upon a shaven head has been known to constitute a very effective motivating stimulus; and the faintest cry of an infant may wake a mother from her sleep.

In addition to the motivating stimulus or condition, there is a "sensory situation," a wider environment, to which the individual may react even while responding primarily to the motive itself. One might even say that an oganism *reacts* to a situation as a whole while *adapting* to but one aspect of it. The responses of a hungry man at the dinner table provide a good illustration. Such a man is not ordinarily oblivious to the table conversation, to a hair upon his plate, or (especially) to the food at the end of his fork; yet it is undoubtedly the hunger-motive that is responsible for his presence in this eating-situation.

Finally, adaptive behavior involves a response that changes the sensory situation and satisfies the motivating conditions. The pain disappears when the splinter is drawn from the finger; the stuffiness of the overheated room is dispelled when the window is opened; hunger goes as food is ingested; the mother turns back to her pillow when the child is comforted—in all these cases an adaptive response has in some manner altered the sensory situation and removed the motivating stimulus.

In addition to these final, "consummatory" responses, which serve to eliminate the motivating conditions more or less directly, adaptive behavior shows an initial, "preparatory" phase.

Consummatory responses are preceded by preparatory responses, and the latter may influence the former in a number of ways. They may (a) induce a state of readiness and alertness that helps the organism to make the final response clean-cut and effective, (b) enhance the effectiveness of the sensory stimulus, and (c) shut out distracting stimuli. Thus, (a) a low moan in the night brings me up on my elbows in bed; (b) I turn my head to listen; and (c) I check my breathing, to avoid even the faint disturbance of its sound. All these attentive reactions are made in preparation for "whatever comes." Further illustrations are unnecessary; the reader will recognize the importance of such adjustments in every situation where motivating conditions may not be immediately or directly satisfied. Even a meal, for civilized man, must be prepared for in some fashion. The actual ingestion of food—a consummatory response—is almost always preceded by reaching, grasping, leaning, and other preliminary movements, as well as those behavioral embellishments that we call "table manners."

We are about at the end of our story of functionalism as a systematic position in psychology. There is much more that might have been said. Carr's text, alone, includes a treatment of the human nervous system and sense organs, of learning, perceiving, reasoning, affection, and volition, of individual differences and the measurement of intelligence. However, the point of view, in its broadest aspects, should be clear to the reader by now. A few concluding remarks will serve to make the picture sufficiently complete for our purposes, and provide a partial résumé of what has gone before.

In spite of the fact that the functionalists professed an interest in the purely "psychical" aspect of mental activity and accepted introspection as a valid psychological method, it is quite obvious that their primary concern was in the physical aspect of such activity and the objective method of observation. Their absorption in animal, child, and abnormal psychology; their interest in mental tests—which, as every student knows, are really behavioral tests; their reverence for the Darwinian tradition; their emphasis upon the usefulness of mental activity; their treatment of the reflex-arc concept; and their notion of adaptive behavior—all these things point in no uncertain manner away from the classical, Wundtian view of psychology as the study of mind or experience, and towards a newer, biological view of psychology as the study of organismic reaction.

Besides showing a wider scope of interest than that in the normal, adult, human individual, functionalism broadened the idea of psychology's subject matter in another respect. In rejecting structuralistic analysis and stressing the complex and continuous interplay of factors in human behavior, the men of this school displayed a willingness to accept the view, now current, that the larger, more meaningful totalities of an organism's activity are fully as important units for investigation as are the more easily measured Titchenerian elements. This is particularly evident in the adaptive-behavior concept, which dealt with a highly purposeful mode of organization. In other words, they emphasized long-term segments of mental activity—events that took appreciable time and possessed a logical beginning and end that gave them their identity. The structuralist's "determining tendency" may have been a recognition of the same thing, but this concept never reached the status for him that "adaptive behavior" did for the functionalist.

Functionalism was, at its best, a loosely knit system and school; and it is this very quality that was at once the strength and the weakness of the movement. As a system it was flexible; as a school it lacked unity. It permitted the inclusion of material from many sources (*too* many, Titchener would have said) in so far as such material was based on sound scientific procedure; but it examined no one's philosophical credentials sufficiently to avoid a confusion of tongues on fundamental issues. It had no single point of view with respect to the mind-body problem and even showed a lack of agreement as to the proper usage of the keyword, function—matters of no great practical importance, but systematic weaknesses that functionalism's critics were not slow in pointing out.

Only in its oppostion to structuralism, its accent upon biological adaptation, and its regard for utility does functionalism stand as a unified movement in the history of modern psychology. Nevertheless, its effect was, in the main, healthy, and it represents a point of view that still has advocates today. If its strength as a school has been hard to evaluate, this is probably due to the fact that *another* school replaced it before it really came of age.

Before the undisciplined forces of functionalism could be brought together along a single front, under one banner, the smoke and fire of a newer and more vigorous attack upon the Titchenerian stronghold came to obscure a great deal of the advance that had been made. This new attack was that of the *behaviorists*, under the able and aggressive leadership of a man whose dislike for the campaign measures of functionalism was only exceeded by his disdain for the guns of structuralism.

9

WATSON
AND BEHAVIORISM

Behavioristic psychology has had several names, not all of them complimentary. In addition to "behaviorism," its most common title, it has been called "objective psychology," "anthroponomy," "stimulus-response psychology," and even the "psychology of the other one"—not to mention such impolite labels as "muscle-twitchism." It has also had many interpreters, but the true founder and promoter of the system was John B. Watson (1878–1958), and it is mainly to a treatment of his point of view that this chapter is confined.

John Watson became acquainted with structuralism and functionalism at the University of Chicago, where he studied under Angell and where he received his doctorate in 1903. His dissertation was in the field of animal psychology. The experiment that brought him his degree was one in which he eliminated one or another sense-organ function in white rats that had been trained, or were to be trained, in running a complicated maze. One conclusion that Watson drew from his experimental results was that the animals relied to a great degree upon kinesthetic cues in their mastery of such a problem— cues, that is, which came from the muscles themselves. It may well be that this conclusion had something to do with Watson's later stress on muscular response in his system of psychology. Little straws of this sort sometimes tell the way the theoretical wind is going to blow.

At any rate, Watson began his professional career with a background of animal experimentation and functionalistic teaching. His first book, *Behavior, an Introduction to Comparative Psychology*, was appropriately dedicated to James R. Angell and Henry H. Donaldson (the latter an authority on the white rat). This book, which came out in 1914, while Watson was a professor of psychology at Johns Hopkins University, contained an early announcement[1] of the behavioristic program. It was followed, five years later, by Watson's best-known text, *Psychology from the Standpoint of a Behaviorist*—a book devoted to human psychology and destined to bring fame to its author. *Behaviorism*, a more popular version of his position, came still later, in 1924.

"Psychology as the behaviorist views it is a purely objective experimental branch of natural science." With this sentence, Watson begins his 1914 text, and follows it immediately with a brief outline of his program. Psychology is to study *behavior* as its *subject-matter*; its *method* is to be entirely *objective*; and its central *problem* is to be one of *prediction* and *control*. These points make up the positive aspect of the new system, and they will be expanded in these pages. There was also a negative aspect, which appears in Watson's criticism of his predecessors, and a few examples will show that he did not mince his words.

"States of conciousness," like the so-called phenomena of spiritualism, are not objectively verifiable and for that reason can never become data for science . . . .

In all other sciences the facts of observation are objective, verifiable and can be reproduced by all trained observers . . . Psychology, on the other hand, as a science of "consciousness" has no such community of data. It cannot share them, nor can other sciences use them . . . Even if they existed, they would exist as isolated, unusable "mental" curiosities . . . .

The psychologist's use of "introspection" as its principal method has been another serious bar to progress . . . . All that introspective

[1] Taken from a paper, printed the year before, *Psychology as the behaviorist views it*. Psychological Review, 1913, 20, 158—177.

psychology has been able to contribute is the assertion that mental states are made up of several thousand irreducible units like redness, greenness, coldness, warmth, and the like, and their ghosts called images, and the affective irreducibles, pleasantness and unpleasantness . . . .

Whether there are ten irreducible sensations or a hundred thousand (even granting their existence), whether there are two affective tones or fifty, matters not one whit to that organized body of world-wide data we call science.[2]

The older psychology, says Watson, had something very esoteric in its methods. Experiments were carried out upon a highly selected circle of subjects, those who were trained in a highly artificial introspective technique. If a subject was unable to experience one to seven degrees of "clearness," for example, he was judged inadequate as an observer; or if he found his "feelings" to be reasonably clear, his introspection was again at fault. The attack is on the observer, rather than the experimental conditions. In physics or chemistry, the latter would be examined, not the former—was the apparatus adequate, were the chemicals pure, etc. "In these sciences a better technique will give reproducible results. Psychology is otherwise."

Furthermore, according to Watson, structural or introspective psychology was fast becoming so concerned with the "true" nature of mind, consciousness, sensations, and so on, that it was degenerating into a field of argumentation rather than experimentation. This deplorable state of affairs was directly attributable to its alleged subject matter and the method of introspection.

Nor were the functionalists, in Watson's opinion, much better off than their unscientific cousins. Although they threw out the Titchenerian elements and pretended to deal with "mental functions," they still employed the introspective method. In addition, they were almost inevitably doomed to fall into some sort of philosophical dualism with respect to their subject matter—either that of interactionism or parallelism. Concerning such positions, Watson had said, as early as 1913:

Those time-honored relics of philosophical speculation need trouble the student of behavior as little as they trouble the student of

[2] J. B. Watson, *Psychology from the Standpoint of a Behaviorist*, pp. 1–3.

physics. The consideration of the mind-body problem affects neither the type of problem selected nor the formulation of the solution to the problem.[3]

These are plain-spoken assertions, to say the least, but very representative of Watson. They are the statements of a young man, defiant of the dogma of structuralism, disgusted with the confusion of functionalism, eager to set psychology free from its philosophical tradition and give it equal footing with other branches of biological science. Whether they were or were not entirely justifiable statements is a question that need not bother us for the moment. Certainly they found many sympathetic ears, particularly in the younger crop of American psychologists, many of whom were already thinking, and some of whom were even writing, in the same vein, although not so forcefully.

Watson founded behaviorism in America and was, for a time, its mouthpiece and promoter. Although he established no formal headquarters comparable to the Cornell laboratory, or even Chicago, he was able, through the simple and colorful language of his books, his lectures, and his popular articles, to catch the fancy of a nation. If his opinions were inconsequential to some and shocking to others, they were, nevertheless, absorbed by all. Structuralism became, in the minds of many, a museum piece, and functionalism was forgotten. His influence spread into the classrooms of the universities and the homes of the literate laity (there were laboratory behaviorists and parlor behaviorists) and it is with some reason that, even today, for some Europeans, American psychology and Watsonian behaviorism are indistinguishable.

No attempt will be made, in what follows, to discuss the systematic views of any early behaviorist other than Watson. The aim in this context, as previously, is to present our major problem—defining psychology—in terms of individual theorists who had vivid ideas on that subject. Such a procedure is questionable, since it focuses attention upon men, rather than the broader developments in which they merely played a conspicuous part; but it

[3] *Psychology as the behaviorist views it.* Psychological Review, 1913, 20, 158–177.

is hoped that what is lost of generalization may be returned in the coin of specificity—that it will be better for the reader to have a rather accurate account of Watson's position than a hazy interpretation of an entire movement.

In 1919 Watson defines psychology as "that division of natural science which takes human behavior—the doings and sayings, both learned and unlearned, of people as its subject matter." He qualifies and expands this general statement by saying that behavior consists of *responses*, *reactions* or *adjustments* of an organism to certain antecedent events—*stimuli* or *stimulus-situations*. We are already familiar with stimulus and response from our discussion of functionalism. The terms were originally physiological, and Watson points out that we must extend their meaning somewhat in psychology to cover more complex, integrated events than those with which physiology ordinarily deals.

We might, he argues, use "stimulus" to designate such simple, measurable things as light rays or sound waves, and "response" for such restricted activities as movements of a muscle or group of muscles; while "stimulus-situation" and "adjustment" might be employed with reference to more complex matters—one's surroundings at a given moment, and one's talking, walking, or other activities. However, "stimulus" and "response" are terms satisfactory enough for either order of complexity, if we remember that we have extended the physiological usage. This is justifiable, moreover, on the grounds that the more complex events of either sort are theoretically analyzable into their simpler components. A *situation*, according to Watson, can be resolved into a complex of stimuli, and an *adjustment* is composed of a group of responses, "integrated in such a way . . . that the individual does something which we have a name for."

Watson's primary interest is in the *response* factor, since that is characteristic of the organism itself,[4] and he shows us two ways of subdividing this category. Physiologically, responses involve the action of "effectors"—muscles and glands. The striped or skeletal

[4] Watson did not, of course, ignore the fact that some stimuli, e.g., the kinesthetic and organic, arise within the organism.

muscles are responsible for all external movements of an organism in space; the unstriped or smooth muscles are concerned with the organism's internal adjustments. The activity of the former is seen in most of our everyday responses, from the crooking of a finger to the rowing of a boat. That of the latter is seen in the responses of the stomach, bladder, blood vessels, and the like. The responses of the glands include the secretion, under appropriate conditions, of tears, sweat, saliva, and so forth.

Psychologically, the responses of these muscles and glands may be conveniently grouped in four main classes. There are (1) *explicit habit responses*, (2) *implicit habit responses*, (3) *explicit hereditary responses*, and (4) *implicit hereditary responses*. "Explicit" and "implicit" are synonymous, respectively, with "overt" and "covert" or "observable" and "non-observable." Within the first class are most of those work and play activities in which humans are daily engaged—"unlocking a door, tennis playing, violin playing, building houses, talking easily to people, staying on good terms with the members of your own and the opposite sex"; in the second class are those smooth muscle and glandular reactions that have been established in us through some degree of training—blushing at the sight of a loved one, sweating at the sound of a dentist's drill; in the third class are "man's observable instinctive and emotional reactions as seen, for example, in grasping, sneezing, blinking and dodging, and in fear, rage, love"; and in the fourth class are included the various gland secretions, circulatory changes, and the like that have been studied in such detail by the endocrinologists and physiologists.

Watson devotes several chapters of his text to an account of these response classes, and we shall have occasion to refer to them in more detail when we consider one or two of the prominent doctrines of his system. For the present, however, we had better employ ourselves with his treatment of the *methods* of psychology.

The *general* method, as mentioned above, is that of objective observation, but there are many *specific* objective techniques, experimental and otherwise, that the psychologist utilizes in his work. These, upon examination, show themselves to belong under one of four main headings: (1) observation, with and without experimental control; (2) the conditioned-reflex methods; (3) the verbal-report method; and (4) the methods of testing.

The first class includes all those necessarily crude observations of man in his everyday world, together with the more refined observations of the laboratory. Thus, we may judge from a subject's reactions to the objects of his common environment that he has some visual or auditory weakness; but only when we isolate, repeat, and vary the conditions of an observation systematically (in other words, perform an experiment) can we arrive at any definite and quantitative statement of the subject's defect. Apparatus and refined techniques (Watson did not scorn "brass-instrument" psychology) should be employed wherever possible to increase the delicacy of our judgments and extend the power of our senses; laboratory study should supplement field study.

The conditioned-reflex methods really constitute special examples of the way in which instruments are used in psychological observation, and Watson's emphasis upon them is illuminative of his scientific background and his objective leanings. He proposes to apply these methods to the study of human behavior as a check upon, or substitute for, the classical procedures, and in studies where language methods are impossible or inadvisable (e.g., with infants, deaf-mutes, and certain "mental-hospital" cases).

In principle, the application of Pavlov's (or Bekhterev's) procedure to the study of sensory capacity in human beings is quite simple. If the muscular or glandular response of an experimental subject can be conditioned to the sound of a given tone, when all other possible cues for his response are eliminated, we may be sure that he is sensitive to such a sound—that he "hears" the tone. With this fact determined, we may proceed up or down the scale of tonal stimuli, by little steps or great, until we learn the *range* of his sensitivity. Moreover, by presenting the unconditioned stimulus (food or shock in our examples) in connection with one tone and withholding it in connection with other nearby tones, we may determine the least noticeable tonal difference that our subject may sense anywhere on the scale. We may find, in other words, the *sharpness* of his sensitivity. And all this may be done without requiring a single word of report from our subject; in fact, when we use the conditioned *secretory* reflex, he may not even know how sensitive he is to these stimulus differences.

A word about terminology is appropriate in connection with Watson's third class—the verbal-report methods. The "observer" of Titchener's experiments is the "subject" of Watson's. Introspective psychology called for an experimenter *and* an observer in laboratory studies. The experimenter set up the essential conditions and the observer reported upon his "experience," a report that was recorded, of course, by the experimenter. In behavioristic studies the true observer *is* the experimenter, who observes, not his "experience," but the *responses* of his subject. The essential subject matter, in the former case, is that which the "observer" describes—namely, his "experience"; in the latter case it is the "observer's" *description*, i.e., the verbal reactions that the subject makes under the conditions prepared by the experimenter.

The verbal-report method is, therefore, the Watsonian substitute for the method of introspection. The difference between the two is a difference of interpretation rather than of actual practice. When, for purposes of expediency, the rather laborious and time-consuming conditioned-reflex methods are not to be recommended, or when the responses cannot be registered other than in the subject's words, the verbal-report methods may be of value. However, because of their inexactitude, they should be used as sparingly as possible.

The *testing methods* need no elaboration here. Watson considers as "behavioral" the various "mental" tests—intelligence tests, special-ability tests, and the like—since the psychologists's real interest, in every case, is in the "doings" (verbal, manual, and otherwise) of a subject with respect to certain test problems. He points out that more emphasis should be placed upon the nonlanguage tests and that we need not treat the tests as unscientific merely because they find so much application in the everyday pursuits of human beings.

The *problem* of psychology, as mentioned above, is the prediction and control of human behavior. Or we may say that psychology is confronted with *two* problems: "the one of predicting the probable causal situation or stimulus giving rise to the response; the other, given the situation, of predicting the response."

Here, perhaps better than elsewhere, we see the reason for the wide appeal of Watson's system. Most human beings would like to know how to predict and control the behavior of others—"to take advantage of others" might be the appropriate phrase in some instances. What reader of this book, for example, would not be willing to spend many hours at his "psychology," if he were certain thereby to enhance his power of social control?

Watson could have said, without greatly misrepresenting his program, that psychology's task was to analyze human behavior into reflex elements, to study the laws of connection of these elements, and show the nature of their dependence upon neural function. He chose, instead, the prediction-control motif—a motif that every one regards as a distinct feature of exact science, and one that has been attractive to man since time immemorial.

In dealing with these problems, Watson points out that, in order to predict the probable causal situation from our observation of some behavioral item, many facts must be at our disposal. For example, the answer to the question "Why do men go to war?" requires a knowledge of (a) man's unlearned response repertory, (b) the various habits he has formed, (c) the tradition of the group to which he belongs, (d) the social conventions he respects, and (e) the effect of such agencies as the church and the school upon his development. Furthermore, these facts themselves can only be acquired through the prolonged application of psychological methods to the study of human behavior from infancy to old age—the so-called *genetic* or *developmental* approach.

The other face of the problem—"given the situation, to predict the probable response"—is equally difficult of solution and demands equally a background of psychological knowledge. But the fundamental answer is the same. We must amass behavioral data through the untiring use of our experimental procedures; and, eventually, such data will permit us to reply, in other than the present hit-or-miss fashion, to such broad social questions as might be raised concerning the probable effect upon human initiative of a certain form of government, or such individual questions as the effect of sudden wealth upon a friend.

This is a large order for psychology, and Watson realized it, but his faith in the experimental and genetic approach to the study of human conduct led him to believe that much could be done in this direction. By studying, in the laboratory whenever possible, the behavior of the infant, the child, the adolescent, the adult, and the senescent—both normal and abnormal—he hoped that psychology might be able to offer expert advice in many practical spheres of human activity.

He was, moreover, not slow in leading the way. His stress upon the genetic method and his interest in both the pure and applied aspects of science are seen clearly in his own selection of experimental problems. One of the best known of his investigations may be considered here as typical of the program that he sponsored.

The distinction between hereditary and habitual responses has already been made, and it has been noted that Watson gave both types extensive consideration in his 1919 text. He was not the first to draw a line between the two. The problem of the *innate versus* the *acquired* was old when John Locke was a boy and René Descartes was writing about "innate ideas." But Watson brought to the study a relatively new point of view. He proposed to settle the question by appealing, not to the behavior of the adult human, but to that of the newborn child—tracing the development of reaction step by step and noting the first appearance of hereditary as well as acquired modes of response.

Scientific studies of infant behavior are not always easy to carry out, mainly because of the objections raised by adults, and parents in particular. Moreover, the validity of some conclusions drawn from such studies has been roundly challenged because of the small number of subjects experimented upon. It is usually unsafe to generalize about the reactions of infants in general from observations made of a single child, or even a dozen.

Watson, while at Johns Hopkins, was able to surmount both of these obstacles by obtaining permission to examine psychologically (as a part of regular hospital routine) several hundred newly born babies at the Harriet Lane Hospital in Baltimore. By means of systematic and almost daily observations it was possible to catalogue, at the time of their appearance, the unlearned responses of infants during the first months—in some cases, years—of life.

Able assistance and a wide range of tests enabled him to collect a great deal of factual material of this sort, a complete enumeration of which need not be undertaken here. In brief, he found a large repertory of reflex activities (sneezing, crying, grasping, blinking, and so on) that appeared in rather well-defined sequence during the early days of infancy; and three types of emotional response (rage, fear, and "love") that "belong to the original and fundamental nature of man."[5]

With respect to these emotional responses, Watson argued that they were each elicited at their first appearance by a restricted number of stimuli. Loud sounds and loss of support evoked the fear response. The blow of a hammer upon a steel bar or the sudden jerk of a blanket from beneath a half-sleeping infant were very effective. The hampering of an infant's natural movements evoked rage. The soft stroking, patting, or manipulating of certain sensitive bodily zones were effective in bringing out the "love" response.

As to the behavior itself, in these fundamental emotions, Watson reported that there were three discernible patterns of response. Fear involved the catching of the breath, tight closure of the eyelids, random clutching movements of the hands, puckering of the lips or crying, and other observable changes. Anger or rage involved such responses as the stiffening of the infant's body, slashing movements of the hands and arms, holding of the breath. While love (Watson asks us to strip the word of its old meanings) showed itself in smiling, gurgling, cooing, and, in older children, extension of the arms—"the forerunner of the embrace of adults."

The more specialized and coordinated emotional display of adults was attributed by Watson to the development and elaboration of these unlearned patterns of infancy; and he maintained that the great variety of objects and situations known to call out emotional reactions in later life were to be explained by reference to the principle of conditioning. He found, for example, that, in spite of

[5] Watson was not the first to catalogue infant reflexes, although he may have worked with a larger number of subjects than his predecessors. The reader may recall David Hartley's list of "automatic motions," mentioned in chapter 4 (p. 25). A more exhaustive set of observations was made by the German physiologist, Wilhelm Preyer, who collected data from his son, three times daily, from the birth of the child until it reached the age of three. Preyer's findings, first reported in 1880, are presented in his famous book, *The Mind of the Child. Part 1: The Senses and the Will*. (English translation by H. W. Brown, D. Appleton, New York 1919.)

much baby lore to the contrary, no fear was shown by infants when presented for the first time with cats, dogs, pigeons, rabbits, and a number of animals at the zoo. This lack of fear response was due, in his opinion, to the fact that the children had not *learned* to be afraid of these things. Even fear of the dark, so common in children, he traced to past experience with loud sounds in the absence of light: "A child that has gone to bed for years without a light with no fears may, through the loud slamming of doors or through a sudden loud clap of thunder, become conditioned to darkness." (John Locke, in talking of the association of ideas, said something in a similar vein: "The ideas of goblins and sprites have really no more to do with darkness than light; yet let but a foolish maid inculcate these often on the mind of a child, and raise them there together, possibly he shall never be able to separate them again so long as he lives; but darkness shall ever afterwards bring with it those frightful ideas, and they shall be so joined, that he can no more bear the one than the other.")

In order to test the validity of this explanation, Watson carried out experiments to determine the possibility of conditioning the fear-pattern to other than the "natural" stimuli. In one of these investigations he used as a subject an 11-month-old infant—"stolid and phlegmatic, but extremely well and healthy"—and combined the stimulation of a loud sound and a white rat, on a number of successive occasions. The child's original response to the rat was of a friendly, investigatory nature; but, after no more than seven combined presentations of rat and loud sound, the sight of the animal alone was sufficient to evoke a strong fear-reaction. "The instant the rat was shown the baby began to cry. Almost instantly he turned sharply to the left, fell over, raised himself on all fours and began to crawl away so rapidly that he was caught with difficulty before he reached the edge of the table."

Moreover, there was a *transfer* of this emotional reaction to a large number of other stimuli. The presentation, a few days later, of a rabbit, a dog, a fur coat, cotton wool, human hair, and a Santa Claus mask was decidedly fear-inducing—in spite of the fact that the infant had previously played with each of these objects at every opportunity. (In this phenomenon, we have the rough equivalent of Pavlov's *generalization*, as well as Thorndike's *response by analogy*—even the associationist's *law of similarity*, but Pavlov's major work was not yet available in English, and Watson was more concerned with breaking new ground than in relating his researches to the past.)

It is through this mechanism of conditioning-plus-transfer, Watson argued, that human beings may be provided, during infancy, with much of their complex emotional equipment, sometimes to their serious disadvantage. All those failures in adult social adjustment—ungrounded fears, unwarranted rages, and unreasonable love-attachments—may have their roots in the emotional upsets and accidents of infancy or early childhood. Likewise, all of the more complicated emotional responses common in adult behavior, to which we give such names as *shyness, shame, hate, pride, jealousy*, and *anguish*, are combinations and permutations of the three elemental response patterns of fear, rage, and love. We may note, in passing, that Descartes, more than two centuries earlier, called for *six* primary emotions—wonder, love, hate, desire, joy, and sadness—from which all others evolved; but his classification, like others before and since, lacked the sanction of experimental and genetic studies.

By this time the reader has perhaps wondered what became of Watson's "stolid" youngster with the transferred fears; or, what is more to the point, whether emotional responses of this sort can be removed as well as implanted. Three years after the studies just reported Watson undertook to answer this question experimentally with another group of children. In this case he selected subjects of different ages, in whom there appeared pronounced fear-responses, of unknown origin but presumably conditioned, and attempted to "*un*condition" them.

The procedure employed in the eradication of conditioned fears was somewhat similar to that used in their fixation. An example will show this. In one experiment Watson chose as his subject a three-year-old boy in whom there was excellent adjustment to ordinary life situations, except for an exaggerated fear of white rats, rabbits, fur coats, and the like. This child was accustomed to taking his afternoon lunch of crackers and milk in a room about 40 feet long. In the tests he was placed at one end of this room, with his lunch before him. At the same time a rabbit, in a wire cage, was displayed to the child "just far enough away not to disturb his eating." This place was marked by the experimenter and, on succeeding days, the rabbit was brought closer and closer to the subject—in each case almost to the "disturbing point." Eventually the child came to eat with one hand and play with the rabbit with the other! In addition, his emotional response to other fear-objects was markedly diminished and, in some cases, entirely eliminated— another example of a transfer effect. No scolding, no coaxing, no compulsion was involved; the careful application of an experimental technique was sufficient.

Watson had, of course, some theoretical statements to make about emotions and their traditional partners, instincts. He defined emotion as "an hereditary 'pattern-reaction' involving profound changes of the bodily mechanism as a whole, but particularly of the visceral and glandular systems." Stated in terms of the four response-categories mentioned above, emotion is basically a matter of "implicit hereditary response" and "explicit hereditary response," with the former predominant.

Instinct is treated, in 1919, as similar to emotion and usually concurrent with it, but more *explicit* (observable), and more adaptive (i.e., better suited to adjust the organism to its external environment). It is also less chaotic in its onset, and less diffuse in its nature. It is defined as "an hereditary pattern reaction, the separate elements of which are movements principally of the striped muscles." (Five years earlier Watson had defined it similarly as "a series of concatenated reflexes," a definition not unlike Herbert Spencer's description of instinct as "compound reflex action.")

Watson's examples of instincts in human infants may, however, be taken as equally good illustrations of reflexes, for he includes such responses as sneezing, yawning, stretching, and nursing. His discussion of the matter emphasizes the fact that instincts are practically impossible to identify in adult activity because of the overlayer of habit responses that hides them from observation. It is not surprising that later, in his popular book, *Behaviorism* (1924), he boldly discards these "hereditary pattern-reactions" and affirms that all of the complex organized behavior of adult humans is a result of the influence of training (conditioning) upon the basic, unlearned beginnings of response (reflexes). Even such early activity as that of crawling and walking is described as a conditioned development of the reflex responses of the arms, legs, and trunk of the child; and handedness (right or left) is treated as a learned, rather than an hereditary, characteristic. Furthermore, it is emphasized that the emotions themselves, although pattern reactions initially, are soon conditioned in many ways that obscure their early unlearned nature.

Watson especially assails, in this book, the idea of inherited "capacities," "talents," "temperaments," and the like. The musician's son who takes up music, the criminal's son who turns to crime, the John Stuart Mill who follows in his father's footsteps, the "chip off the old block" in every walk of life—all are the result, not of hereditary, but of *environmental* factors. Says Watson:

> Give me a dozen healthy infants, well formed, and my own specified world to bring them up in and I'll guarantee to take any one at random and train him to become any type of specialist I might select—doctor, lawyer, artist, merchant-chief and, yes, even beggar-man and thief, regardless of his talents, penchants, tendencies, abilities, vocations, and race of his ancestors.

This proposal to throw out instinct from psychology came as a shock to many of Watson's readers. Some, who liked its implications, were heartily sympathetic; others, who did not, were equally antagonistic; but both groups were impressed. They were so impressed that, even today, in the minds of many, John Watson, behaviorism, and the denial of instinct are all one.

Watson had other startling things to say—other novel proposals with reference to age-old psychological problems. One of these deserves attention here because it illustrates further the scope of his system and answers a question that might seem, to the reader, unanswerable from a behavioristic platform. The problem is that of the nature of *thought*; the question, "What is thinking?"

Thinking, in the Watsonian scheme, falls under the heading of "implicit habit response" and is primarily a matter of "language" activity. Language, however, is not entirely confined to vocal responses (laryngeal or voice-box reactions), but includes movements of a gestural sort—for example, the shrug of the shoulders, the wave of the hand, the wink of an eye. Thinking differs from talking in being implicit rather than explicit, covert rather than overt; it is, in a very real sense, subvocal talking and subgestural gesturing, and it may even involve widespread reactions, provided that these reactions have become conditioned to serve as substitutes for other reactions or stimuli.

Watson offers various types of evidence to support this position. The child who "thinks out loud," but who is reduced by parental admonition first to whispered and finally to silent response; the none-too-socialized persons who, when alone, whisper or speak their "thoughts" or move their lips in reading; the deaf-mute who talks and thinks (even dreams) with his fingers—all these may be taken as proof that thinking and talking (or gesturing) are one and the same.

Watson presents other evidence, often of a direct, experimental nature, to show that implicit response and thought may be identical, but the inclusion of this material here would bring us into a controversial field and certainly would not alter *his* view of the matter. Neither need we consider his treatment of the various stages or degrees of thinking—from the mere unwinding of language habits to the trial-and-error solution of difficult problems. The general doctrine should be clear; thinking is response; the response is predominantly verbal; and its final result is adjustment of the human organism to a complex social environment.

We have already considered the Watsonian system with respect to the subject matter, the methods, and the problems of psychology; and we have sampled its investigations and concepts. The remainder of this discussion will be in the form of broad characterizations aimed at giving the reader an opportunity to compare the system with those I have previously outlined.

First of all, behaviorism, in the hands of its founder, tended to stress cross sections of human conduct, rather than its long-term aspects. In spite of his emphasis upon genetic studies and past history, Watson's main concern was the simple stimulus-response relation, regardless of what had gone before or, especially, what came after. Watson's preferred experimental model, one might say, was that provided by Pavlov's dog, rather than Thorndike's cat.

In this respect, the system resembles structuralism, with its accent upon momentary mental contents or processes. There was little in the Watsonian portrayal that might have been likened to the functionalist's stress upon stimulus-response interplay or the concept of "adaptive behavior." The bodily *set* or *orientation* was not yet in the foreground of behaviorism, even to the degree that Titchener's "determining tendency" was a feature of structuralism. *Urges, drives, motives,* and *organic needs*, which later became so prominent in psychological literature, were scrupulously ignored by Watson, possibly because of their historical association and identification with the instinct concept.

Secondly, like Titchener, Watson was an elementarist in psychology. He held that the complex personality of an individual is built up from a large number of very simple unlearned response elements through the process of conditioning; just as Titchener argued for mind as a fusion and combination of mental elements, joined together, at least in great part, through the principle of association. This elementarism was not so explicit in Watson as in Titchener because of the former's emphasis upon the end appearance of such combinations—the integrated, response groups rather than the members of such groups—but it is obviously a significant phase of his systematic position.

Thirdly, notwithstanding the fact that, in Watson's 1919 text, he presented a rather elaborate account of the nervous system from a purely anatomical and physiological point of view, it is clear that he was not so much interested in the more or less hypothetical "mechanism" of behavior as he was in the behavior itself—the observable acts and adjustments of the organism with respect to its environment. In 1924 he states in outright terms that the nervous system has been little more than a "mystery box" for the introspective psychologist: "whatever he couldn't explain in mental terms he pushed over into the brain." Watson proposes to give this system no more status than any other part of the response mechanism—in his own words, "to place no more emphasis on the brain and spinal cord than upon the striped muscles of the body, the plain muscles of the stomach, the glands, etc." Moreover, he points out that the adjustments of the *whole* organism are more significant for the behaviorist than the workings of *parts*; and his distinction between the behaviorist and the physiologist is based largely upon the latter's concern with specific bodily functions such as digestion, respiration, and circulation, whereas the former "works with the whole body in action."

Finally, the practical slant of this system exceeds even that of functionalism. This should already have been evident to the reader in the discussion of "prediction and control." The questions that Watson posed for psychology were always questions of a common-sense nature, the answers to which everyone would like to know. Moreover, he conceived it to be the duty of experts in psychology to lend hands in many places—in advising parents, educators, law-makers, and businessmen; in helping the individual organize his own life activities and in helping society progress in its knowledge and control of thy individual. In contrast with Titchener, who described the scientist as disinterested and impersonal—devoted to facts rather than values—Watson never divorced observation from application; he was as ready to use a fact as to find one. Titchener would have called Watson a technologist rather than a pure scientist; and Watson would not have minded!

Many arguments have been launched against behaviorism and many epithets have been hurled at its founder. The system has been called materialistic and mechanistic because it had no place for *consciousness, mind, soul, volition*, and kindred concepts; and because it sought a natural-science explanation of psychological matters. It has been criticized as crude, illogical, naïve, and subversive—even "anti-psychological." Watson himself was accused of oversimplifying psychological problems; of forcing mental categories into physical pigeonholes; of producing theories that could not be verified; of supporting an untenable position in the eyes of philosophy, medicine, law, religion, and ethics; of making art meaningless; and of corrupting the youth.

Into the truth or falsity of these accusations we need not here inquire. Some of the issues raised were pointless and irrelevant; others were not, and will receive some consideration in a later chapter of this book. There is a warlike literature that the reader may consult if he desires, but it is not always an enlightened literature. Strong emotion does not further the best in evaluative judgment, and Watson elicited many angry responses.

However, it should not be assumed that Watson lacked supporters. The philosophers, psychologists, religionists, and writers who assailed behaviorism were met by other, equally aggressive gentry who came to its defence. It was as often hailed as a panacea as it was a poison, with as much (or as little) justification. The real strength of a system, however, is not measured by the heat of its first skirmishes or the clamor of camp followers.

The heyday of Watsonian behaviorism was exciting, but it could not last for long. The freshness of its appeal was bound to fade in the public eye as the public fancy turned to other things, and as serious-minded students of psychology began to examine the system in a contemplative fashion. Other behaviorists, more academically-disposed contemporaries and successors of Watson, came forward to advance the general program; but there were many cautious reservations and well-considered modifications. The viewpoint, under the pressure of its critics, was clarified, qualified, and broadened in its scope. Now, in its tailored form and in more sober colors, it nearly suits the customer for whom it was intended—the experimental psychologist of the 20th century.

Whether behaviorism grew to its full size, blossomed, and then withered, may be a matter for historians to settle. Whether it absorbed psychology or was absorbed by psychology is, perhaps, a question for the future. Whether its immediate effect upon psychology would have been greater without the advent of another, strikingly different, but equally disturbing point of view will never be known. My own judgment on these issues will have to be postponed—at least for another chapter—while attention is given to a system that grew up with behaviorism, and the subtle foreign charm and dramatic qualifies of which nearly eclipsed for a time all other attempts to formulate a definition of our science.

10

GERMANY
AND GESTALT

In 1912, Titchener, the structuralist, had just seen his *Textbook* printed in German; Angell, at Chicago, was publishing his third exposition of functionalism; and Watson, at Johns Hopkins, was preparing to shout the battle cry of behaviorism. In that year there appeared in a German psychological journal a report, from the University of Frankfurt, of some *Experimental Studies of Apparent Movement*. The writer was Max Wertheimer (1880–1943), and the two principal observers in the experiments he described were Wolfgang Köhler (1887–1967) and Kurt Koffka (1886–1941). The report itself marks the beginning of a new psychological system—a system of which Wertheimer was to be called the founder, and Köhler and Koffka the chief exponents.

"Gestalt" psychology was a purely German product and we had best adopt the German name for the school.[1] Translations of *gestalt* are sometimes employed—*shape, pattern, form, structure,* and *configuration* have all been suggested as English equivalents—but none have been quite so acceptable as the German word itself, for reasons that require no presentation here.

---

[1] In this text the word "gestalt" will be capitalized only when it refers directly to the *school* or *system*; and "gestalten" will be used as the plural of "gestalt."

Like functionalism and behaviorism, Gestalt psychology arose in the form of a complaint. Functionalism complained about structuralism; behaviorism complained about structuralism *and* functionalism; and Gestalt found fault, to a greater or less extent, with the concepts of structuralism, functionalism, *and* behaviorism. It seems as if the remark of David Hume was no less applicable in 1939 than it was in 1739: "Nothing is more usual and more natural for those, who pretend to discover any thing new to the world in philosophy and the sciences, than to insinuate the praises of their own systems, by decrying all those, which have been advanced before them." Certainly Gestalt psychology did much decrying, particularly with respect to structuralism and, a little later, behaviorism, and there were two or three principal hypotheses that it attacked with especial vigor.

The first protest was against the doctrine of elementarism in psychology—the belief that mind (or behavior) is a mere collection, mosaic, or "bundle" of elementary units. A doctrine of analysis into elements we have already observed in Locke, Hume, and the Mills—father and son; in Wundt and Titchener; and, to a degree, in Watson. The nature of the elements subscribed to have varied from Locke's *ideas* to Watson's *reflexes*, but with practically no exceptions, theorists have favored some form of elementary analysis since the very beginnings of psychology.

The Gestalt attack was leveled primarily at that form of "bundle hypothesis" sponsored by Titchener and, less explicitly, by Watson. The charge against Titchener was that sensations, images, and feelings are *not* the raw materials out of which mind is built, but are the products of the highly sophisticated technique of introspection, which destroys the object of description to leave a handful of elements "which nobody ever sees." Watson was similarly condemned on the ground that behavior is *not* a combination of reflexes, either original or conditioned, but that these units are established through "bit by bit" observation which has regard only for easily registered but insignificant facts, leaving the more important aspects of activity untouched.

The second major complaint of the Gestalt school was against the "associationistic thesis"—a doctrine that developed alongside of elementarism and was closely related to it. Association, as we have seen, supplied the mental glue that held the elements together—the mortar for the psychic bricks. Since, to the Gestalt psychologist, the elements themselves were artificial, the connections between the elements were bound to be equally so. Their criticism was aimed not only at the mental mechanics of James Mill but the mental chemistry of his son, and all of the later modifications of the doctrine—even the behavioristic principle of conditioning. The *organization* that characterizes all experience or behavior was *not*, according to these critics, to be explained by appeal to connections or bonds. The whole problem was, to them, a false one, arising from a mistaken view of the nature of analysis.

Some of the logical and experimental justification for these criticisms (and related ones) will be clearer as we proceed. There are two outstanding systematic treatments of the Gestalt point of view—Köhler's *Gestalt Psychology* (1929) and Koffka's *Principles of Gestalt Psychology* (1935)—both of which contain many assaults upon rival schools and many specific examples of their failure to meet psychological reality. Gestalt was a closely knit school and these two texts are in rather complete accord on fundamental issues.

Neither book, however, is easy reading, even for the specialist in psychology. The terminology is markedly different from that of structuralism, functionalism, or behaviorism, and the point of view, coming out of a philosophical and scientific tradition that I have been compelled to neglect in this historical approach, may seem disturbingly novel to the beginning student.

Psychology is defined by Koffka as *the study of behavior in its causal connection with the psychophysical field.* This definition, however, requires considerable qualification if it is to be distinguished adequately from those with which we have already concerned ourselves in this book.

First of all, there are to be differentiated two kind of behavior: *molar* and *molecular.* The simple reflexes of Watson's studies—what Koffka calls "relatively isolated movements elicited by relatively isolated stimuli"—and the reflex arcs of the 19th century physiologists—those rather sharply defined nerve paths over which an excitation passes from sense organs to muscles or glands—are considered by Koffka as examples of *molecular* behavior. *Molar* behavior, on the other hand, is taken to include such things as riding a bicycle to work, attending a football game, or carrying on a flirtation.

This distinction between molar and molecular may remind the reader of Watson's distinction between *adjustment* and *response*; but Koffka points out that molar behavior is by no means to be thought of as analyzable into a number of molecular elements. Furthermore, a fundamental difference (for Koffka) between molar and molecular behavior is that the former takes place *in an environment*, while the latter occurs *within an organism* and "is only initiated by environmental factors called the stimuli."

Psychology is to study molar behavior; and molar behavior occurs in an environment: the bicyclist wheels along the avenue; the football fan's activity takes place in the crowded stadium; and the flirtation occurs in a suitable, essentially social, atmosphere. Moreover, *two* kinds of environment may be distinguished, in but one of which, strictly speaking, behavior may take place. There is a *geographical* and a *behavioral* environment; and Koffka tells us a story to illustrate the difference between them.

A lone horseman, according to a German legend, arrived one wintry night, after long hours of riding over a wind-swept and snow-covered plain, at the door of an inn where he sought warmth and shelter. The innkeeper, obviously surprised to see him, asked him from what direction he had come. The traveler replied by pointing out his route. The innkeeper, more astounded than ever, told him that he had ridden across the thinly frozen Lake of Constance; whereupon the traveler, overcome by the shock of the discovery, fell stone dead at the innkeeper's feet.

Geographically, says Koffka, the traveler of this legend rode across a lake; behaviorally, he crossed a plain. In everyday language the horseman "thought" he was riding on solid ground but "really" he was passing over thin ice. His behavior was behavior-with-respect-to-a-plain, rather than behavior-with-respect-to-a-lake; the Lake of Constance was his geographical, the plain was his behavioral, environment. The behavioral environment, although determined in part by the geographical environment, was not identical with it. One might even say that it was the geographical environment taken *from the traveler's point of view.*

What holds for Koffka's legendary horseman would hold for all of us in all of our activities. Except in very rare cases, our behavior is regulated directly by a behavioral environment, and only indirectly by a geographical one. The bicyclist may ride along the same (geographical) avenue as the motorist who passes him; the loyal fan who cheers loudly for one football team may share his bench with an equally ardent supporter of the other, and the partners in flirtation may "carry on" in the same drawing room. In each case the two behavioral environments have much less in common than the geographical, and they are much more significant with respect to the reactions that are evoked.

The reader who has followed this carefully will perceive that Koffka's behavioral environment is not Watson's *stimulus-situation*, but comes closer to being Titchener's *experience.* A glance back at Koffka's definition of psychology—which shows that behavior is to be related to a *psycho-physical field*—will also make it clear that this behavioral environment, since it "causes" behavior, must have something of the nature of the psychophysical field.

The behavioral environment *does*, for Koffka, constitute an important part of the psychophysical field, but the latter really includes a great deal more. It comprises, in addition to the behavioral environment, the awareness of certain other things: "desires and intentions, . . . successes and disappointments, . . . joys and sorrows, loves and hatreds," as well as one's own actions. To return to our horseman: besides his knowledge of the behavioral "plain" and his other "external" surroundings, there was, perhaps, a desire to press on, an annoyance at having lost his way, and an awareness of the stiffened, cramped action of his own muscles and joints as he sat in his saddle. Only when we add this material to the behavioral environment do we have the totality of a subject's consciousness or, as Köhler called it, *direct experience.*

It must now be shown why even direct experience is not the complete equivalent of the psychophysical field in Koffka's definition. This will amount to a demonstration that there are other causes of behavior than those of which a person is conscious; and I shall select three examples to make the point for Gestalt—three specimens of behavior that have no conscious determinants.

(1) If, into the eyes of a boxer knocked unconscious, a bright light is thrown, the pupils of the eyes will still contract. (2) A bachelor, once jilted within the hearing of his own wedding bells, has a strong dislike for bells, which he traces to their musical imperfection. (3) An experienced telegrapher, with his ear to a sounder, copies a message on the typewriter before him, while indulging in a friendly chat with a fellow employee.

These are samples of three types of behavior determinants considered by Koffka as being outside the direct experience of the individual. The boxer did not know that the light was causing his pupillary reaction, nor would he have known if he were "conscious"; the bachelor's explanation of his dislike for bells convinces no one that it was the real cause; and the telegrapher's ability to carry on two tasks at once is not to be attributed entirely to rapid fluctuations of attention, especially since he may be unable to report the content of the message copied during the conversation with his friend.

Reflexes, unconscious determinants, and certain aspects of memory and skill—these are the classes into which our three examples fall. They are types of behavior that demand the inclusion of more than conscious forces within the psychophysical field. If the reader wonders why reflexes, previously treated as molecular behavior, are mentioned here, it is because Koffka finds a place for them as *field-determined* in his system. The complete field will consist of *external experiences* (the behavioral environment), *internal experiences* (desires, intentions, etc.), and other forces which have no status in experience at all.[2]

Koffka's definition requires still more elaboration. The Gestalt psychologist argues that direct experience itself is closely paralleled by neural, especially brain, activity; the organized consciousness of a person is a true representation of a corresponding organization in the underlying physiological processes. These underlying processes,

---

[2] *External* and *internal* are not Koffka's terms. They are used here as convenient shortcuts to avoid developing another set of distinctions in Gestalt that would not greatly enhance the value of the present account of the system.

however, must be thought of as fundamentally molar in their nature, not molecular as in the Wundtian or Titchenerian system. These brain processes are not considered to parallel mental elements or to cause simple-reflex responses, but to represent larger, better-integrated *wholes of experience* or *gestalten* and to cause equally well-integrated totalities of action.

We know about these molar physiological processes, according to Gestalt theory, just as we know about a person's direct experience, although we may not always be able to state the exact nature of the processes in a way that would satisfy the physiologist (particularly the 19th century physiologist). From the consideration of direct experience, together with the unconscious determinants above-mentioned, we build up our notions of these physiological events, just as, in fact, we construct the geographical (physical, stimulus) environment. We find organization in the physiological, as well as in the physical, world because of a fundamental organization of direct experience. Only a brokendown physics and an outworn psychology could, in the opinion of Gestalt psychologists, find anything else.[3]

We may go even further. Since language is the symbolic mechanism in humans for telling about their organized experience, it may serve at once as a symbol of the physiological and, less directly, the physical or geographical reality: "if, to me, my language is an adequate symbol for my own direct experience, it is an objective symbol for those physiological processes at the same time" (Köhler, 1929). When there is no language, as is the case with animals, some other form of behavior will do just as well. Says Köhler: "The behavior of a chick can tell me without words that he is able to react to one brightness in relation to another. If in the course of an experiment, a human subject tells me that he sees one object as brighter than the other, the scientific value of this sentence is exactly the same as that of the chick's behavior."[4]

One important word in Koffka's definition still awaits our attention. It is a word that indicates the major emphasis of Gestalt

[3] The Gestalt view that the basic, dynamic structure of consciousness is the *same* as that of the related physiological events is called *isomorphism* (equal in form).

[4] Wolfgang Köhler, *Gestalt Psychology*, 1929, p. 69.

psychology and is almost synonymous with *gestalt* itself. This word is *field*; and Koffka was the one who probably used it most. Outside of *organization, field* is perhaps the most frequently encountered systematic term in Koffka's book.

Koffka tells us that in physics the concept of "action at a distance" of objects upon one another has been supplanted by the notion of "fields of force" in the medium between the objects; that the physicist now speaks of electromagnetic and gravitational fields and holds that the distribution of stresses and strains in the environment of an object with a given constitution will determine what that object will do. Likewise, a knowledge by the physicist of what the object does will tell him the properties of the object's field. For instance, the movements of magnetic needles tell about the magnetic field of the earth, while the movements of pendulums tell of the gravitational field.

"Can we introduce the field concept into psychology, meaning by it a system of stresses and strains which will determine real behavior?" The answer to this question is already known to the reader, who knows also, from what has gone before, just what the field will include. He may not know, however, of the dynamic stress-and-strain character which Gestalt ascribes to this psychophysical field. I shall offer, later, experimental examples that will demonstrate this character in several ways, but a few everyday observations may be taken from Koffka as particularly illustrative.

How often have we seen the beginning cyclist come to grief against the only tree or telephone pole in an otherwise vacant lot? How often does the novice at hockey or soccer drive his puck or boot his ball squarely at the body of the goalkeeper who stands stock still between the enemy posts? More often, we say, that is accounted for by chance; and Koffka would warmly agree! He would say that there are, in a behavioral environment of the kind in these examples, "things" and "holes" between them; and the former are more compelling and attractive than the latter. The things are centers of force, so to speak, that determine the behavior. Until the rider or the player learns better, i.e., reorganizes or reconstructs his behavioral world, he will react to the things rather than the holes.

These are examples of the dynamic quality of the behavioral field, and there are many others of a similar sort, but Koffka's point should now be clear. The reader should appreciate to a greater degree the intrinsic nature of the psychophysical field as the Gestalt psychologist treats it; and he should see why the static, bundle concept of experience could never have appeal for the members of this school.

For the last time we turn back to the Gestalt definition of psychology, "the study of behaviour in its causal connection with the psychophysical field," with the aim now to review what we have learned. We have seen that the behavior studied is to be molar (large, organized totalities) rather than molecular (small, isolated elements) and that molar behavior takes place in (is caused by) a behavioral environment—which is the geographical environment as the organism views it. We have seen that when certain other experience, of a more subjective nature, is added to this behavioral environment, we have the equivalent of direct experience or consciousness; and we have found out that, in addition to direct experience, there are "unconscious" factors that go to complete the psychophysical field. Furthermore, it appears that, wherever knowledge permits, we may substitute molar physiological processes for the direct experience of the psychophysical field; and, in any actual experiment upon human or animal subjects, we may find out about the nature of these processes from language or other behavior. Finally, we have had a glimpse of the meaning of "field" in the Gestalt system.

It is tempting to boil all this down to a one-sentence formula, stressing the view that the physical (geographical) environment causes molar, dynamic events in the nervous system that give rise in turn to molar behavior. However, this would be to neglect the direct experience that goes along with some of these physiological changes and which was, to the Gestalt psychologist, the starting point of his science. Moreover, Koffka himself says that, although the members of this school aim one day to talk in physiological rather than experiential terms, it will be convenient for some time yet to use purely psychological language—although this language must not be that of Titchener or Wundt.

After this much of an introduction to the Gestalt system, and following the same procedure we adopted in connection with the three preceding systems, we may ask: What was the subject matter, and what were the methods and problems of Gestalt psychology?

Our answers have been given, at least in broad outline, in what has gone before, but it will do no harm to restate them.

If we choose to call the subject matter *behavior*, Koffka will tell us that we can know about behavior only through our own experience of it; if we choose to call it *experience*, he can point out that experience—at least the experience of another person—is known only through behavior. If we say *experience and behavior*, he can argue that we are ignoring other important events. Perhaps we had better say *behavior as determined by psychophysical processes* and hope, by thus approximating his own definition, to win Gestalt approval.

The *method* of Gestalt psychology seems at times to be that of direct observation and at times that of introspection. Yet it is not the kind of direct observation that finds reflex units, nor the kind of introspection that discovers mental elements.[5] We shall see, later, with specific examples, what kind of behavioral and experiential phenomena the Gestalt psychologist encounters when he uses each method, and this will help us to understand the methods themselves.

The *problem* of Gestalt psychology is to determine the intrinsic nature and organization of the psychophysical field and to study its relation to (a) the geographical environment and (b) the behavior that results from the field organization. It aims also to "explain" direct experience by reference to the underlying, purely physiological, field.

From the very outset, Gestalt was a productive system experimentally. Although this is no place for a comprehensive treatment of these matters, a few specimens may be selected as indicative of certain interests of the school and as illustrative of its protest against the structuralistic and behavioristic points of view.

The initial experimental study of the school was, as mentioned at the beginning of this chapter, an investigation, by Wertheimer, of "apparent movement." Since no other Gestalt experiment has been referred to more often in psychological literature, a brief review of

[5] The sort of introspective observation used by Gestalt psychologists is called "phenomenological," by which is meant "as naïve and full a description of direct experience as possible"—as opposed to a kind of description "which analyzes direct experience into sensations or attributes or some other systematic, but not experiential ultimates."

this classic research is appropriate here, even though Wertheimer's work has been greatly developed and expanded by other scientists, both German and American, in more recent studies.

If two electric lights are placed a few feet apart along one edge of a table and an upright rod is put on the other edge between the lights and a nearby wall and equidistant from each light, two shadows of the rod may be perceived on the wall. Now, if the lights are switched on and off alternately, in rhythmical succession and at the proper rate of speed, the shadow of the rod will appear to move back and forth between its two positions. When the time between the two light exposures is too short, the shadows will appear simultaneously each in its own place; when the time is too long, there will be merely a succession of shadows—first one and then the other, in their respective places. In neither of these extreme cases will movement of the shadows appear, but various degrees of apparent back-and-forth movement of the shadows may be observed as the time interval between the successive turnings on of the lights approaches an optimum, which, for Wertheimer's experiment, was about sixty milliseconds (.060 sec.).[6]

The reader is undoubtedly familiar with things similar to this in everyday life, particularly in the compelling movement-portrayal of various electric signs where, commonly, each bulb provides a single dot of light but what one sees is a moving streak. And then there is the smooth motion of modern moving pictures (an invention, incidentally, based upon the psychological studies of a Belgian physiologist more than a hundred years ago). However, Wertheimer was not trying to reinvent or improve upon such devices; he was interested in more fundamental scientific matters—the "How?" and the "Why?" of apparent movement.

After Wertheimer had gathered his experimental facts, he undertook to explain them. Obviously, the movement that his subjects reported was "subjective," since there was no "real" movement; the movement occurred in the "behavioral" rather than the "geographical" environment. However, there were no current explanations of

---

[6] Wertheimer employed a more refined technique than the one outlined here, but it was the same in principle.

the phenomenon which seemed to do justice to the actual experience. Wundt had argued that kinesthetic sensations, produced by the quick movements of the eyeballs as the subject glanced from one stimulus to the other, might provide the cues for movement perception—just as Berkeley had argued that other eyeball sensations gave us our criteria for judging the *distance* of an object from us. Wertheimer, however, was able to get clear-cut reports of movement even when *two* pairs of stimuli were used simultaneously, one calling for movement in the *opposite* direction to the other, and where the time taken for the presentation of both stimulus pairs was less than the time required for the eyeballs to react to a single pair.

Other explanations were found to be equally unsatisfactory. Wertheimer concluded that no solution of the problem could be reached in terms of simple sensations conceived to be good representations of simple physical objects (stimuli) or simple unitary neural processes. Moreover, he was not satisfied with the idea of calling the movement an illusion or attributing it to the influence of past experience or "meaning." He believed that it was as real an experience as any other and just as worthy of psychological attention—that it was an experienced *totality* and was not to be reduced to some combination of elementary sensations, held together by no matter what sort of "mental glue."

Using Koffka's terms we might say that Wertheimer's position is that the behavior environment is not related point-for-point with either the geographical environment or the underlying physiological events. (The name given by Gestalt psychologists to that theory which *supports* a one-to-one correspondence between specific stimuli and specific sensations is the *constancy hypothesis.* Wertheimer's results, of course, argued against this hypothesis, as well as the previously mentioned *bundle hypothesis.*)

In order to emphasize the unique "gestalt" nature of movement observed where physically (geographically) there was none, Wertheimer named it the *phi phenomenon* and undertook to investigate it in its own right. The explanation he arrived at was *isomorphism*, referred to in an earlier footnote of this chapter. Apparent movement—a dynamic, unified *whole* of experience—was interpreted as due to a similarly organized *whole* in the brain processes. Molar phenomena were explained, that is, by reference to molar physiological events which had a structure that paralleled the mental structure in its properties. Wertheimer dismissed the traditional notions of neural function, with their stress upon the compounded activity of tiny anatomical units, and assumed instead the existence of "cross-processes" in the brain and its attached organ, the eye. Only in this way was he able to understand the perception of movement when there was no movement in the stimulus situation itself. The perception was held to be the result of a dynamic organization within the nervous system—an organization that took place naturally under the proper conditions of stimulation.

This has been a basic type of argument in Gestalt psychology ever since. Let us take another example from the study of visual perception to make the point clearer—the problem was raised by Bishop Berkeley when he sought to explain how we perceive the distance of objects from us.

The third dimension of space, according to Berkeley, "of itself and immediately, cannot be seen. For, distance being a line directed endwise to the eye, it projects only one point in the fund [retina] of the eye, which point remains invariably the same, whether the distance be longer or shorter." He went on, as we have seen, to enumerate the various cues or criteria used by us as signs of the distance of objects, thus giving a solution to the problem that was satisfactory to psychologists for a great many years.

Gestalt questions Berkeley's answer and then denies its validity. Koffka points out that Berkeley made two false assumptions in the statement I have quoted. First, he assumed that, since the retina of the eye is two-dimensional, our visual perception must also be two-dimensional, merely giving knowledge of up-and-down in space, or right-and-left, but not of far-and-near. Secondly, he assumed that one could know about the visual field adequately from a study of the *points* in it.

The second of these assumptions is, for Koffka, little more than the affirmation of the constancy hypothesis, which he denies on the basis of such experiments as Wertheimer's upon apparent movement. The first assumption fails to consider that the sensitive surface of the eye, which is two-dimensional, is really but a "boundary surface" of the brain, which is *three*-dimensional. Why, then, Koffka asks, could not this three-dimensional brain be related *naturally* to three-dimensional experience? He concludes that it could, and offers a number of experimental observations to show that three-dimensional space is even *more* naturally perceived than two-dimensional space, that the perception of a *surface* (which is what Berkeley started with) is really a later development in visual experience than that of depth.

Koffka does not appeal, as Watson might have, to the genetic development of space perception in humans, but he brings forth evidence from the reactions of adults to various portrayals of three-dimensional objects (e.g., the picture of a wire framework in the form of a cube), which is taken to show that the appreciation of depth is really a more primitive form of organization than surface perception. Moreover, he uses other experiments to show how various stimulus conditions, including the cues or criteria of the older psychology, might be used to help or to hinder this natural function.

A single example of these experiments will illustrate the ingenuity of the Gestalt attack. Suppose that under the same circumstances in which apparent movement is reported, there be presented, in rapid alternation, a v-shaped figure and, directly above it, an inverted-v (so placed that, if both were presented at once, a not-quite-closed diamond would be seen). What kind of movement will result, under optimal conditions? Will there be movement of an up-and-down nature, causing a distortion of the figure in a two-dimensional plane; will there be some sort of motion around the vertical axis within the plane of the drawing; or will there be a rotation in the third dimension around the horizontal axis?

The reader is predisposed, by the way in which the problem has been stated, to reply that the third possibility is the most likely one; and he is right, although the other two types of movement occasionally occur. The most common report is that of a wheel-like rotation around the horizontal axis—a rotation in the third dimension of space! In other words, third-dimensional movement appears in the behavioral environment when there is no movement, not even two-dimensional, in the geographical.

Experiments of this sort have been very puzzling to those psychologists who have followed in the Berkeleian tradition and tried to show how depth perception is built up in a spatial world that has little or no depth to begin with. Moreover, such experiments possess a broader significance than that which bears upon this particular problem. They illustrate the manner in which old problems, even "dead" ones, are often revived in science with the application of new methods and new points of view.

My two examples of Gestalt research have been chosen from the studies made upon the visual portion of the behavioral environment. The most original and provocative, as well as the greatest number, of this school's investigations were made in the field of visual perception. Yet it should not be concluded that the other senses were entirely neglected or other chapter headings ignored by the members of this group. Gestalt aimed to throw light into every hidden recess of psychological thought and to demonstrate the value of applying Gestalt principles to every type of psychological function. Koffka's book, to which I have referred so often, contains, in addition to chapters on the "environmental field" of the organism, chapters on *action, memory,* and *learning* as well as a chapter on *society and personality* with which he ends his lengthy exposition. Everywhere the treatment is permeated with the same point of view; everywhere *organization* is stressed, whether it is organization of the visual field, of the *Ego*, or of the neural traces underlying memory. Everywhere, in the examination of experience or behavior, gestalten appear—i.e., organized totalities of experience or behavior which have definite properties not traceable to parts and their relations.

The most characteristic theme of Gestalt psychology, that the whole is more significant than, and determines the nature of, the parts that compose it, is brought out in ever so many contexts within Gestalt literature. Even the colors of everyday objects, the notes of a heard melody, the sequences of habitual or instinctive action are shown to be dependent upon the spatial or temporal structure of which they are parts. For example, a white paper in deep shadow still seems white and a black paper under direct illumination holds its blackness, in spite of the fact that the actual intensity of light reaching the eye from the two surfaces may be the *same.*[7] Likewise, coal looks black in the sunlight when the (geographical) stimulus energies ought to make it look white; and a plate in the middle of a dinner table still appears round although more often seen otherwise, i.e., elliptical. A dancer may execute a difficult double shuffle, yet be unable to demonstrate the parts of the step; and an ape may portray the hunger instinct with never the same muscular components. Gestalt consideration of the "whole" has even provided some justification for judging character from handwriting and photographs—procedures long since discredited by the elementaristic type of research that dealt with measurements of letters and other details and with isolated facial features.

There are many more concepts and configurational (gestalt) laws that were developed by the members of this school, particularly in their treatment of perceptual matters; but these belong to a more detailed account of the system than this one pretends to be. A few additions to the picture may, however, be made in considering some of the charges brought against the system by its critics.

The indictments of Gestalt have been numerous, but they were, in general, more academic in their nature than those of Watson's behaviorism. They were mostly "intramural"—in spite of the fact that Gestalt professes to be closer to everyday and common-sense reality than either behaviorism or structuralism. Whether this was due to agreement with, or ignorance of, Gestalt precepts on the part of the general public in Germany or America may be a question, but it is likely that the latter was the case. In spite of the almost religious zeal of some Gestalt psychologists, and notwithstanding a dramatic character which their studies sometimes take on in classroom presentation, the problems and experimental interests of the school were of too technical a nature to arouse the widespread discussion that was stirred up by Watsonian pronouncements.

Gestalt psychology has been accused of denying its ancestors and ignoring its contemporaries—of failing to recognize the historical

---

[7] A simple test of this sameness, offered years ago by Helmholtz, may be made by looking at the two surfaces through a peephole in a gray cardboard—thus excluding the "normal" surroundings of the papers. Under such conditions the approximate equality of the brightnesses appears.

roots of Gestalt doctrine and of attacking views, outmoded since the days of James Mill, to which no up-to-date structuralist or behaviorist would subscribe; of substituting vague new terms for well-defined old ones; of supplanting one form of elementarism with another; of accepting the "form" and rejecting the "content" of behavior and experience; and of assuming that "organization" is its own explanation.

A case in point is that provided by Köhler's famous studies of problem-solving behavior in the chimpanzee (*The Mentality of Apes*, 1925). These investigations, conducted by Köhler while interned on a West African island (Tenerife) during World War I, were hailed by many as a great step forward in experimental technique and theoretical interpretation within the field of learning.

Köhler's method commonly required that a hungry chimpanzee, in order to obtain food, must reach his objective by a *round-about* (the German word is *Umweg*) route, by the use of some tool, or even by the construction of some device from the familiar objects of his environment. Köhler's aim was to present his apes with problems that would let them demonstrate their intelligence or "insight"– something more than simple trial-and-error learning as described by Thorndike.

According to Köhler, "insight" learning might be seen as a suddenly initiated, smoothly continuous performance, following a preliminary survey by the animal of the entire experimental field. Thus, an ape showed insight when, after leaping and clutching in vain for a basket of fruit suspended above him, he paused, looked about his yard, and then, in a quick and purposeful manner, dragged a nearby box into position, and jumped from its top to draw down the prize. Insight was also said to be shown when a subject, presented with fruit outside the bars of his enclosure, used a stick to rake it within his grasp; or when, with a stick to short to reach the food, he raked in one that was longer, and used the latter to reach his objective.

The Mentality of Apes was a popular book, and clearly furthered the cause of Gestalt. It was widely read and met with much approval, especially by those who felt that Thorndike's account of learning, and Pavlov's, left much to be desired. Ultimately, however, Köhler's studies also drew fire. Their originality was questioned, mainly by reference to Hobhouse's earlier work in a similar vein (see pp. 55—56). Their status as true experiments was denied, since no identifiable variable was related systematically to any other in any of Köhler's examples; and they were likened to crude intelligence tests, in which the relative contributions of heredity and environmental history could not be determined. As for "insight," the critics argued that Köhler, having defined the concept in behavioral terms, then used it to explain the behavior itself. The path of the innovator in the realm of scientific method is sometimes rough and thorny.

It was stated earlier in this book that we are bound to *analyze* whenever we describe an object or event. Later, we learned that Gestalt psychology began with a protest against analysis, at least analysis of the Titchenerian stripe. Still later, we found that the school was criticized on the ground that it substituted one kind of analysis for another. The fact of the matter seems to be that, in their earlier attacks upon other schools, the Gestalt theorists somewhat overstated their position. Köhler, more recently, denied that the system had no place for analysis, but contended that Gestalt analysis finds more natural (molar) units than those of structuralism or behaviorism. He admitted, moreover, the possibility of an 'artificial' (molecular) analysis itself, as long as it is recognized that the elements arrived at are not really observable in experience or behavior.

We may close the book of Gestalt. It has been a difficult one to read (or reread), but perhaps it was worth the candle. Gestalt was an important step along the way to our goal—psychology's definition. The intrinsic merits of the system; the novelty and significance of its experimental support; the inspired and able missionary work of Köhler, Koffka, and others—all these factors led to widespread recognition of the movement. The very "gestalt-character" of the school, with its dynamic, purposeful organization and its "whole" more important than its "parts" or members, seems to have been responsible for its importance in the history of our science.

Like the structuralism of Titchener, Gestalt was consistent and self-contained; like the functionalism of Chicago, it was flexible and broad; like Watsonian behaviorism, it was healthy and aggressive; and, like each of these viewpoints, it failed to stamp, as its very own, the psychology of today.

11

HORMIC PSYCHOLOGY
AND PSYCHOANALYSIS

If a student of psychology, in the early 1920s, had gone to Cornell University, he could have heard the structuralistic theme, as sketched by Titchener himself, dressed in his Oxford gown. At the University of Chicago, he would have met with functionalism, taught by Harvey Carr. At Johns Hopkins, without doubt, he would have heard about behaviorism and John Watson's studies of infant reflexes and emotions. And if his daring had led him to cross the Atlantic, he might have learned about Gestalt—at Giessen, from Koffka, or with Köhler at Berlin.

If he had gone to Harvard, he would have found a structuralistic bias, sprinkled with lectures on the other schools, mainly as they were given by visiting professors, including Köhler and Koffka. At nearby Clark, he could have had behaviorism with Professor Hunter, as well as structuralism with Professor Nafe.[1] At Columbia, he would have been exposed to *eclecticism*—a middle-of-the-road policy

[1] Walter Samuel Hunter (1889–1954), who later went on to Brown University, was an important figure in the movement from Watsonian behaviorism to the doctrine in its modern form. John Paul Nafe (1888–1970) was one of Titchener's best-known pupils and for many years a teacher in the structuralistic mold.

that tolerated every point of view, but sponsored none.[2] This was a period of competing doctrines, vivid leadership, and hot-blooded allegiances; and veterans of this war may be forgiven today if, on occasion, they reenact the old battle scenes or revive the ancient grudges.

In addition to the points of view already treated in these pages, there were some with fewer credentials—less success in winning converts, or lacking in breadth of systematic coverage. *Hormic*[3] psychology, for example, was never as influential as any of the schools that we've discussed. Yet, William McDougall (1870–1938), its British-born leader, was an outstanding figure of his day, with views that find their parallels in several modern themes.

McDougall was part of a special tradition—one that stemmed from Aristotle and found its classic expression in the teachings of Franz Brentano (1838–1917), a German philosopher, theologian, and psychologist in the days of Wilhelm Wundt. Brentano held that psychology's realm was that of *mental acts* or *functions*, specifically those of *ideating, judging,* and *loving-hating.* He argued that if one looked into his own mind in a natural, common-sense, or "empirical" manner, he would never find *images* or *sensations*—the sort of *content* found by Wundt; instead, he would discover *imagining* or *sensing*—i.e., *acts* of *ideation.* And so on.

At several removes from Brentano in the historical succession, McDougall nevertheless reflects his teachings. He too finds acts of three main classes. There is *cognition* (sensing or knowing), *affection* (feeling or "emoting"), and *conation* (willing or striving). He places most of his stress, however, upon conative action, the purposive endeavor of organisms to reach their goals.

McDougall's views, as presented in his *Outline of Psychology* (1923), had much in common also with those of functionalism. This

[2] The Columbia position was best represented in the teachings of Robert Sessions Woodworth (1869–1962), one of the best-known and best-loved psychologists of this century. He was not himself a "school man," in spite of functionalistic coloration, but his scholarly and sympathetic portrayal of different points of view, in his *Contemporary Schools of Psychology* (first published in 1931), is still worth reading by historically-minded students.

[3] From the Greek, *hormao*, meaning *to urge* or *to impel. Purposive* is alternately used as a name for the system.

is understandable, on two main counts. Act psychology was itself a sort of functionalism, dealing more with mental function than with content; and McDougall was greatly influenced by William James, whose teachings were "functionalistic" before there was such a school. An example of this is found in McDougall's treatment of "instinct" (the motive power of conation), which has much in common with Harvey Carr's account of "adaptive behavior" (see pp. 79–80).

In a sense, McDougall was also a behaviorist, although he spent a lot of time in fighting Watson. He once defined psychology as "the positive science of the conduct of living creatures."[4] Behavior, however, was not for him a matter of reflexes and reflex combinations, as Watson stated. In his *Outline*, McDougall says that *true* behavior has six characteristics that reflex behavior lacks. (1) *It shows spontaneity.* It need not be elicited by a stimulus, although it often is. (2) *It may continue in the absence of any stimulus that started it off.* A squirrel, treed by a dog, may continue in its flight when the dog has passed from sight or hearing. (3) *It shows variability.* "When an animal persists in the movements initiated by a sense-impression, its movements are not predictable in detail." The running of the dog or of the squirrel, in our example, would never be exactly reproduced on successive encounters, although a similar end result might be achieved. (4) *The varied activity ends when the aimed-for result is achieved.* The squirrel ultimately ceases his flight and resumes his daily round of occupations. (5) *True behavior often shows preparatory movements.* The dog may crouch before rushing his prey, or the squirrel may sit up alertly before taking off. Finally, (6) *true behavior shows the elimination of useless movements with practice.* On repeated runs, both the dog and the squirrel improve in their efficiency—as by terminating the pursuit or the flight at an earlier point.

Regardless of the rightness of wrongness, or even the newness, of McDougall's argument, one thing is pretty clear. He approached a fundamental distinction, with which the reader is already acquainted, between reflex and voluntary movement. This was something that Watson had missed, probably because of an

---

[4] William McDougall, *Physiological Psychology*, 1905.

understandable fear of admitting such terms as "spontaneity" and "volition" into natural-science description. Such words often seem to imply a state of affairs in which events occur without a natural cause—a situation that science abhors.

A second noteworthy feature of McDougall's account was his emphasis on the *serial* nature of behavior as we ordinarily observe it. His examples are never of single responses to single stimuli; rather, they are acts in succession. Within the succession, McDougall thought he saw "purpose" (another term that raises scientific blood pressure), but we may accept the *fact* of serial response without reading into it any hypothetical "goal-striving."

Still a third point. McDougall saw *variability* in performance, even in highly routine acts. To some psychologists, like Watson, who aimed to predict the exact response of an organism to each specific stimulus in its environment, this sounded like an admission of defeat. To McDougall, it was merely an acceptance of observed fact. Today, we can see that Watson was too demanding and that McDougall, perhaps, was not demanding enough. Variability at one descriptive level, as when we describe the muscular involvement in successive writings of one's name, may co-exist with predictability that the name will be written under prescribed conditions. Much depends on what we define as a response.

Further into McDougall's formulation we need not go. His viewpoint reached America at a time when every effort was being made to develop psychology as a natural science, modeling it on older, better-established disciplines. Often he seemed to be pulling in the wrong direction. He criticized Watson and other objectivists at a time when they were most in favor. He thought he saw mind or purpose within or behind behavior. He conducted an experiment that seemed for a time to support Lamarck's well-known theory of the inheritance of acquired characteristics. He even sponsored such questionable enterprises as those of "psychic research."

All this made for so much unpopularity that his positive contributions did not get the attention they deserved. Yet, he was a man of great ability and wide scholarship, in such diverse fields as those of social, abnormal, and comparative psychology, not to mention the related fields of philosophy, ethics, and antropology.

His breadth of interest was exceeded only, perhaps, by that of his idol, William James. In another land, or at another time, he might have fathered a more successful school.

Strictly speaking *psychoanalysis* was never a *school* in the sense of the word as it is used within this text. Neither its founder, Sigmund Freud (1856–1939), nor any of his followers ever aimed to draw together all the facts of psychology within a coordinated whole like that of any of the systems we have covered here. Only in the sense of their adherence to a *method of therapy* or a *theory of personality* can the exponents of psychoanalysis be said to have formed a school. Although it grew up with these other systems, it was not a part of any academic tradition. It had its roots in clinical observation and curative technique, rather than systematic discussion or laboratory science. Also, in spite of exercising considerable influence upon academic teaching and experimentation, it has never in turn been seriously affected by developments within this field.

A Viennese neurologist-turned-psychiatrist, Freud's "psychology" changed from time to time, initially as a result of observing patients' behavior, and later in the interests of constructing an integrated picture of the human *psyche*, from infancy to old age and death. The "system" he arrived at had points in common with several of those to which the present reader has been introduced. Like behaviorism, it was *deterministic*, with no response lacking in its natural cause, and in which the important causes were unconscious. Like functionalism, and the Darwinism from which it stemmed, it stressed the adaptive or *adjustive* aspect of behavior, and did not always draw a line between the physical and the mental. Like structuralism, its focus was upon the *individual organism* and the general laws that govern its behavior—a focus that we also find in modern reinforcement theory (chapter 12). Finally, as in the teachings of McDougall, it found behavior's motivating power in the *instinct*.

Instincts were treated by Freud as inborn states of the human being which give direction to such processes as thinking, perceiving, remembering, and the like. They have their source in bodily tissue, from which comes the energy for those actions that will finally fulfill their aim—the removal of excitatory states and bodily needs.

Such a treatment resembles Harvey Carr's account of *motives* (p. 80) and can be found in more recent theorizing, such as that of Hull (see chapter 12), but Freud's elaboration went much further than anything before or after.

Instincts were classified, for example, into those of Life and Death. The former included *sex* (aimed at species preservation) and *ego* (aimed at preservation of the self); the latter were directed toward destruction, either of oneself or others. (Hunger, thirst, and other commonly accepted *drives* of laboratory study were placed by Freud among the *ego* instincts.) With this as a foundation, Freud built up a highly-integrated, often-changing, and controversial account of human development and personality structure. But these are matters that we cannot cover here.

Efforts to bring Freud's thinking into the domain of natural science have taken several forms. First of all were animal experiments, designed to provide the analogues of such psychoanalytic "dynamisms" as *regression, repression, displacement,* and *fixation.* In effect, these studies aimed to produce, usually at the animal level, psychoanalytic "symptoms" and to suggest their origins in the learning process, rather than in war between hidden elements of the personality, such as the *id,* the *ego*, and the *super ego.* Thus, *regression* was used to describe a white rat's return to an earlier means of escaping electric shock when a later one no longer worked; and *displacement* was said to be shown when a rat's aggression toward another rat was turned to some inanimate object (e.g., a celluloid doll) not formerly a cause of such behavior.

Another attempt amounted to an emphasis on parallel conceptions. Freud's *Pleasure Principle* (we aim to avoid pain and to seek out pleasure, and we *learn* to reduce our painful tensions, even by neurotic symptoms) was treated as no more or less than Thorndike's Law of Effect; the Freudian *id* (the primitive, unconscious, "animal within us," which seeks immediate gratification of the Instincts of Life and Death) was seen as the equivalent of hunger, sex, and other animal drives with which the research work deals.

Still other efforts had a two-fold purpose: to advance our basic understanding of behavior through experimentation and to extend the conceptual reach of psychoanalytic teaching. Numerous studies of *anxiety* (a central Freudian theme) in the 1940s and the 1950s illustrate this dual trend.

In general, these endeavors were not without success. They helped to bridge the gap between those concepts based on clinical observation and those derived from laboratory study. Some of Freud's ideas quickly found a home within the teachings of such objectively oriented thinkers as Guthrie, Tolman, and Hull (see chapter 12). Many of them appear today within a context of conditioning, extinction, punishment, generalization, and related areas of modern reinforcement theory.[5]

Freud's place in history is established, but not easily described. As already noted, he was not a "school man"—not even a psychologist by profession. Nor was he simply a psychiatrist who, in trying to cure his patients' disorders, discovered a therapeutic method (*free association*). He was a theorist who tried "to infer or to guess how the mental apparatus is constructed and what forces interplay or counteract in it."[6] More than this, he was versed in literature and the history of culture, in anthropology and religion, as well as Darwinism and philosophy (he translated a volume of the works of J. S. Mill). In a long, productive life, he brought his theories to bear in many of these regions, and he left his imprint on the 20th century in many different ways. His role in helping to define our science was not a leading one, perhaps, from a systematic or experimental point of view, but his effect upon our province as a whole, and in certain special areas of study such as those which have been mentioned here, can hardly be denied.[7]

[5] B. F. Skinner's *Science and Human Behavior* (1953), in which Freud's name appears with greater frequency than any other, provides an excellent *rapprochement* of psychoanalytic thinking to that of present-day behaviorism.

[6] E. Jones, *The Life and Works of Sigmund Freud*, 1953. Vol. I, p. 45.

[7] For the uninitiated reader, a good book on Freudian theory, especially in its relation to the general field of psychology, is Calvin Hall's *Primer of Freudian Psychology, 1954.*

12

LEARNING THEORIES AND THE NEW BEHAVIORISM

Schools of psychology no longer exist as they did in the 1920s. They were quietly ushered out as psychologists turned from argument and debate to laboratory science. In the 1930s and the 1940s, developments in the field of animal learning led to more restricted (and more productive) theorizing, and paved the way to modern definition.

Among the best-known names within this period was that of E. R. Guthrie (1886–1959). An excellent statement of his position can be found in *The Psychology of Learning* (1932; rev. ed., 1952). Taking off from Pavlov's principle of conditioning, Guthrie stressed the contiguity of *stimulus and response*, rather than the contiguity of *stimuli* (conditioned and unconditioned), as described by the famous Russian. Guthrie's basic tenet was that "a combination of stimuli which has accompanied a movement will on its recurrence tend to be followed by that movement."

This so-called *contiguity theory* drew much of its strength from photographic records of the behavior of cats in escaping from a special kind of problem box, not unlike the ones that Thorndike had earlier employed. It was skillfully extended by Guthrie in a series of books and papers, to interpret many cases of human and animal behavior, yet it never led to much experimental research or general acceptance. Not that it was shown to be *wrong*, but that its appeal was less than that of rival formulations.

A more elaborate and productive view than Guthrie's was the cognitive type of theory described by E. C. Tolman (1886–1959), in his *Purposive Behavior in Animals and Men* (1932). This formulation, once described by its author as a kind of "purposive-gestaltic behaviorism," garnered most of its support from experiments with rats in mazes—many experiments and many kinds of mazes. It was a bold and imaginative attempt to escape what Tolman felt to be the narrowness of such accounts of learning as those proposed by Watson, Thorndike, Guthrie, and others. It was also meant to be a *system of behavior*, composed of various interdependent concepts, rather than a collection of unrelated facts or the application of a single principle to many complex cases.

Tolman tried to build his system firmly on experimental data, but was willing to assume the existence of certain "intervening variables" —variables that lay between those of the stimulus situation and those concerned with response. These intervening variables were described as *cognitions, purposes, expectations*, and the like, but Tolman didn't think of them as mental, or even physiological. He preferred to treat them as conceptual, or *neutral*, in their nature—as "processes which interconnect between the initiating causes of behavior, on the one hand, and the final resulting behavior itself, on the other."

Learning, for Tolman, consisted of changes in "knowledge" of the environment, of what leads to what, of what will be rewarded or punished under certain prevailing conditions. In the maze, for example, a white rat develops a *cognitive map* rather than a series of specific movements in response to a specific stimulus sequence. What the animal *does* (his performance) is use his knowledge (what he has learned) in order to attain his ends.

Much of the argument and research that centered about Tolman's cognitive theory related to the scientific need for inferring maps, hypotheses, expectancies, and so on, in order to account for the observed behavior. Tolman argued that they were essential; his critics disagreed. More often than not, they suggested, Tolman's intervening variables were simply mental causes in disguise. Experiments conducted from his point of view were regularly met by experiments from the opposition, usually in long succession and with no final resolution. Even today, the issue is not so much resolved as it is neglected.

Reinforcement theory signifies, for psychologists today, one of two different but related points of view with respect to learning and to psychology in general. One of these is associated with the name of C. L. Hull (1884–1952) and is best known, perhaps, as the *hypothetice-deductive* theory of learning. The other is associated with the name of B. F. Skinner (1904–   ) and has been called *descriptive behaviorism* or, more recently, *radical behaviorism.*[1] The two positions are alike, however, in having reinforcement as their central theme.

The Hullian system will be treated lightly here, for two main reasons. Through its very nature, it presents an ever-changing and highly complex picture, not easily described *in toto*; and, as a system of behavior, it never drew as many followers or had as lasting an effect as did its rival. It was a source of interest for many students in the 1930s and the 1940s, to whom it offered a fresh and appealing approach to the problems of behavior, but as a theory or a method of research, it did not long outlast the passing of its dynamic sponsor.

The most readable introduction to Hull's system is to be found in his *Principles of Behavior* (1943). In this account, he brings together nervous-system physiology, conditioned-reflex study, Darwinian theory, Thorndike's Law, and the model of deductive science provided by Sir Isaac Newton. Defining theory as "a systematic deductive derivation of the secondary principles of observable phenomena from a relatively small number of primary principles or postulates," he then presents, in both verbal and mathematical form, a set of 16 postulates, together with theorems and corollaries, with which psychology may deal.

---

[1] *Operant conditioning*, often used to specify the viewpoint, is too narrow in its connotation; *the experimental analysis of behavior*, suggesting Skinner's method, is clumsy as an expression, but is commonly employed.

These postulates need not be treated here, except for part of No. 4, which deals with reinforcement: "Whenever an effector activity and a receptor activity occur in close temporal contiguity, and this is closely associated with the diminution of a need or with a stimulus which has been closely and consistently associated with the diminution of a need, there will result an increment to a tendency for that afferent impulse on later occasions to evoke that reaction."[2]

The reader cannot fail to be reminded here of Thorndike's Law and all of its antecedents (see chapter 5). There is a stimulus situation, a response, and an effect. But, in place of a "satisfying state of affairs," this effect is *need-reduction* or *stimulus removal*—supposedly a more objective, or potentially more objective, designation. Hull comes closer, perhaps, to Harvey Carr (pp. 79—81) than he does to Thorndike.

The "diminution of a need" takes place, we may assume, *within* an organism, and its presence must be *inferred*, since it cannot be observed directly. This points up the fact that Hull, like Tolman, was not averse to intervening variables in the explanation of behavior. But the "constructs" that he inferred were mainly *physiological*, as suggested by the terms *receptor, effector,* and *afferent impulse* in the above quotation.

Hull's place in modern psychology is difficult to assess. His system, through its very nature, was subject to continual change, not only due to laboratory findings (which were many), but to lively interchanges with the members of his famous seminars at Yale, where he taught from 1929 until his death. His pupils went in many directions, some to eminence within our science,[3] but very few along the trail which he had blazed. His writings are commonly sampled in present-day teaching, especially at the graduate level, but

[2] Clark L. Hull, *Principles of Behavior*. New York: Appleton-Century-Crofts, 1943, p. 178.

[3] Notable among these are Neal E. Miller, at Rockefeller University, an authority on the physiology of behavior, and E. R. Hilgard, at Stanford University, one of psychology's best-known writers on general and systematic matters.

rarely covered in full.[4] Research within the Hullian format, although still cited with respect, is gradually decreasing in its flow. Yet, there is no doubt that Hull's unwavering empiricism, his high regard for mathematical rigor, his devotion to experimental science and his willingness to be guided by its outcome, together with the inspiration and direction he provided for his pupils, won for him an honored place in psychology's hall of fame.

As learning theory developed, in the hands of men like Guthrie, Tolman, and Hull, it came to encompass more and more of the concerns of psychology as a whole. Or, better, the more it became a self-sufficient *system* of behavior, rather than a patchwork of unrelated fact and disconnected concepts. This is vividly apparent in the work of B. F. Skinner, in which the change was carried to its limit.

Skinner's contribution to the definition of psychology was sketched in outline for his colleagues in *The Behavior of Organisms* (1938), a book devoted to the systematic presentation of experimental data which the author had collected in a series of investigations with a new research procedure between the years of 1931 and 1938. In this treatise may be found not only a merging of historical trends with which the present reader is already acquainted but also a program of research and study on which the author himself was to build an illustrious career.

In Skinner's now-famous book, the reflex story was continued from the place where Sherrington and Pavlov left it, but with the elimination of all physiological reference and with a corresponding stress upon *observable* data—stimulus-response relations in which each element was observed and measured. Of the 24 "laws" of behavior discussed by Skinner, at least 15 were treated within a different context in *The Integrative Action of the Nervous System*

---

[4] An outstanding exception to this statement is the critical review by Sigmund Koch in *Modern Learning Theory* (1954), by W. K. Estes, Koch, and others. Professor Koch took 169 carefully reasoned pages for an account of Hull's position in its various phases of development up to the point of its last expression.

(see pp. 26–28), and four more were Pavlov's contributions.[5] All these, however, were included within a systematic whole in which there was also a place for Thorndike's Law of Effect and several other principles which gave to "voluntary" behavior and "trial-and-error" learning as much experimental-science status as was already possessed by reflex action. In fact, the emphasis of the book is really not on reflex or stimulus-elicited behavior (which Skinner calls *respondent*), but on behavior of the "voluntary" sort (he calls it *operant*) which acts upon and alters the outside world.

This emphasis grew out of Skinner's own researches—from his development of a new experimental method and his exploitation of it. Beginning with a study of eating behavior in the laboratory rat, he was led to invent a "repeating problem box" and a cumulative recording device which displayed the rate at which a hungry animal would depress a little lever to produce the pellets of food that made up its daily meal. With such equipment, and with *rate of response* as a measure of the strength of voluntary (operant) behavior, an enormous field of research was opened up for exploration. Many new experimental questions could be asked, and answered.

It was possible, for example, to study the early change in rate, from low to high, when each press on the lever was followed by the food-reward (would the change be sudden and "insightful," or would it take place gradually as Thorndike might have argued?). One could also ask about the change in rate of a well-entrenched response when food was *discontinued*. Or when food was given for pressing the lever in the presence of *one* stimulus (e.g., a light), but not in the presence of another (e.g., darkness). Or if food came only after stated *periods* of responding (e.g., at 5-minute intervals) or after a certain *number* of responses (e.g., 20). Or if responses of a certain *force* were followed by reward, but weaker responses were ineffective.

From the answers to these questions, Skinner came to the principles of *Type R conditioning* (his nearest approach to Thorndike's Law), *Type R extinction*, and *Type R discrimination.*[6] In addition, he introduced the study of *intermittent reinforcement* (see below); carried out experiments on the *differentiation of response* (providing a fresh approach to the classical field of skill); investigated several "drives" (hunger, thirst, activity) in their relation to response rate; and, most significant of all within the present context, drew all these matters together within a systematic framework.

Operant conditioning and extinction, for example, were involved in intermittent reinforcement, and could be alternated with each other as desired. The effect of long-term schedules could be studied and the problem of behavior *maintenance* could appear, replacing that of *acquisition*, which had been the main concern of those who worked with learning in any of its various forms.

Another combination of conditioning and extinction, together with *induction* (generalization), showed itself in Skinner's law of operant discrimination—a law that had its counterpart in Pavlov's system (see pp. 31—32). Still another was represented in his treatment of the differentiation of response, wherein one variation of an act is reinforced and another is extinguished until, through successive approximations, the aimed-at form is finally achieved. In such instances as these, the economy and fruitfulness of behavior theory were portrayed in a manner than had never been achieved before.

More than this, the explanation of behavior was no longer placed within the nervous system, the mental life, or at the door of any other "inner agent"; it was sought and found, instead, within environmental situations, past and present—"in a frame of reference," Skinner said, "provided by the organism itself or by various external objects. . . ."[7] The *criteria of mind*, so long a subject of discussion and conjecture, from Darwin's day to Watson's, therefore had no place in Skinner's system; nor did the *intervening variable* figure in his thinking.

---

[6] *Type R* was used by Skinner in order to suggest the dependence of reinforcement on *response. Type S* was intended to suggest dependence on the *stimulus,* as in Pavlovian pairing of a bell with food (the reinforcement). As terms, *Types R* and *S* did not catch on with students of behavior, and are seldom heard today. *Operant* and *respondent* are more common.

[7] B. F. Skinner, *The Behavior of Organisms.* New York, D. Appleton-Century Co., 1938. p. 6.

The system, nevertheless, was incomplete. *The Behavior of Organisms* contained a blueprint only of the structure that was later to result from the efforts of its author, his pupils, and those colleagues who were drawn to his position. Skinner, himself, was soon to lead the way in several directions. In the laboratory, he extended some of his earlier researches and developed new procedures. He carried reinforcement theory into the field of human speech and language, with a new and thought-provoking treatment which broke away completely from the dualistic view of language as a means of expressing one's "ideas." He wrote an introductory textbook, wherein various classical concepts (*sensations, images,* etc.) were given fresh interpretations, psychoanalytic dynamisms were given behavioral meanings, and most of the major topics of psychology were represented. In addition to all this, he took his analysis from the laboratory to the fields of educational practice and cultural design.[8]

Skinner's method was adopted first by workers in the field of animal behavior who saw the possibility of prediction and control, with individual subjects, to a degree that never had been realized before. Some of these investigators merely sought to use the method for purposes of their own, but others undertook research with systematic implications, aiming to extend or test the limits of the original formulation. A few attempted to determine its utility at the human level.

As a result of such endeavors, Skinner's brand of reinforcement theory expanded far beyond its 1938 expression, both in the realm of basic science and of its application. Textbooks were written and courses were designed to expound the viewpoint and instruct in laboratory practice; a journal was founded for the publication of experimental studies, to be followed by another which dealt with useful applications; and a society was formed to further the scientific and professional interests of the group.

---

[8] The books that Skinner wrote, or helped to write, in connection with these topics, may be listed here, in the order of their mention: *Schedules of Reinforcement* (with C. B. Ferster, 1957); *Verbal Behavior* (1957); *Science and Human Behavior* (1953); *The Analysis of Behavior* (with J. G. Holland, 1961); *The Technology of Teaching* (1968); and *Walden Two* (1948).

It became, in fact, a behavioristic system, with some of the features of the older school, and others that were new. It was one in which laboratory research took the place of polemic and debate; in which experimental data led the way, inductively, to a coherent group of laws (a system), without the aid of any "hypothetico-deductive" process. It was one in which functional relations (of stimulus, response, and reinforcement), pertaining to the individual organism, occupied the center of the stage; in which *reinforcement* meant the presentation or removal of some stimulus, rather than reduction of a drive. It was one in which determinism was accepted as the scientific way of life, mind-body dualism was rejected, and hereditary causes of behavior were assigned a minor role, pending further exploration of "environmental" limits. Finally, it was one in which the *understanding* (or explanation) of behavior was tantamount to its *prediction* and *control.*

13

THE PROBLEM
OF DEFINITION

It has been asserted (p. 21) that "a system of psychology is, in a sense, nothing more than a logical framework into which may be fitted the findings of the science." The schools and learning theories treated in the last six chapters of this book may be considered as support for such a statement. In each case, the author of the viewpoint attempted to present a logically interrelated and comprehensive set of facts and principles within a unitary whole.

In another sense, a system can be called an elaborate *definition.* It determines or fixes the boundaries of a science at the same time that it clarifies its meaning. Titchener told us, for example, that psychology was the science of the "mind," then tried in great detail to clarify the meaning of that term. "Mental activity" was expanded on by Harvey Carr, and "behavior" by John Watson; and Koffka's text was an extension of "behaviour in its causal connection with the psychophysical field." The kind of introductory definition given in each instance had to be worked over and extended to its limits before the point of view could *really* be defined; and this comprised the system.

System may be viewed in still other ways than these. When many seemingly different facts can be brought together and related to a few established laws, our task of thinking about these facts, or even calling them to mind, is easier than it was before. System is a simplifier, an economizer, and a memory device. It also helps us to estimate the importance of each fact with which we deal, just as we judge the structural importance of a building's parts.

When the laws themselves are interrelated, a system can provide a power of interpretation and evaluation which may, in turn, give rise to profitable research or successful application to practical affairs. The unity in multiplicity which system can achieve may even be described as beauty.

The systems of psychology that existed in the 1920s were poorly integrated and uncertain in their scope. They were based on little data and generated little more. Except in psychophysical studies and in some of the investigations of Gestalt, the experimental models were extremely crude in both equipment and procedure. The maze, the problem-box, the *Umweg*, and other learning methods, for example, almost never generated useful data, or data that could be confirmed by later workers. The situation with respect to such topics as emotion, thought, and motivation was even worse than that for learning. The identification of experimental variables in other than the sensory area was practically unknown. Interest in environmental causes of behavior was less, it would appear, than in hypothetical causes which resided in the nervous system or the mind.

In the 1930s and the 1940s all this changed, as researchers in the field of learning, as well as some from psychophysics, began to sharpen their perceptions of what could be observed and what could only be inferred among the variables with which they dealt. Psychological terms came to be more carefully defined by reference to experimental procedures (operations) that were connected with their use. *Hunger*, for example, was defined exclusively by specifying objective conditions (e.g., food deprivation) that preceded the measurement of certain responses (eating, salivating, approaching food, etc.). Mentalistic concepts in particular underwent a fresh examination. *Sensations, images, feelings*, and the like lost their old subjective reference. Rather than ask about *red* as conscious process, one asked about the circumstances under which "red," a verbal response, was uttered.[1]

This culminated, as we have seen, in Skinner's *reinforcement theory* (*theory* is here meant to be synonymous with *system*) or *radical behaviorism*, which is in fact our only thriving system of behavior at the present time. Indeed, it is perhaps the only system of *psychology* presently supported by any appreciable number of natural-science workers in our field.

This is not to say that most psychologists today are radical behaviorists, or advocates of any other theory. Systematic interests seldom occupy the center of the stage in any science, and the definition of psychology is, rather curiously, not of serious concern to most of those who work within our province. Some see themselves as *methodological* behaviorists, agreeing that their measurements may be of stimulus and response, but clinging to their inference of "mind" and its underlying physiological function, just as Wundt did long ago. Still others—perhaps the great majority—will accept whatever orientation their problems of research have historically possessed. Their interest is in special topics rather than an overview, and system sits but lightly on their shoulders.

The systematic bias of the present writer must be obvious to the reader: the most satisfactory definition of psychology today is that of radical behaviorism. Such bias may have been apparent quite early in this book. The "history" of a science is in part determined by what we believe the science is right now; the *present*, in a sense, *selects its past*. Descartes' distinction between reflex behavior and that dictated by the soul would be of little interest without the acceptance of two classes of behavior (respondent and operant) in psychology today. Neither Titchener nor Watson would have thought it worthy of attention.

[1] This change in attitude was furthered by *operationism*, a widespread movement against metaphysical explanation in science, which was much discussed within the period considered here. Professor Tolman even went so far as to call his system "operational behaviorism."

This reference to history suggests two further statements that should be made in connection with the viewpoint here endorsed. First, this system is incomplete and still undergoing change. Thousands of experiments have been conducted since 1938, when Skinner first outlined its salient features. New facts have been gathered, methods have been improved, emphases have shifted, and a few new areas of study have appeared. There is every reason to believe that comparable developments of the system lie ahead.

Secondly, and finally, some entirely new formulation may appear—one with wider acceptance and greater appeal than modern reinforcement theory or any of its antecedents. The history of science is a history of growth and change. The data that result from further research may not easily fit within the present system, and drastic alterations may be needed. That prophet must be bold indeed who tells us that our present system of psychology will bear any likeness to the system that obtains 100 years from now.

INDEX

145